FOREX TRADING

CURRENCY TRADING MADE SIMPLE

THE ULTIMATE FOREX GUIDE FOR BEGINNERS

SECRET STRATEGIES, TIPS AND TRICKS

MARK STOCK

Table of Contents

Introduction

Welcome to *Forex Trading*!

In this book, I'm going to explain the exciting world of currency trading to new and aspiring traders.

If you are just discovering Forex, you might be asking the ultimate question – why trade currency instead of stocks or options?

There are several reasons. The first reason to trade Forex is that it's global. There are currency traders worldwide and as a result, currency trading takes place 24 hours a day on business days. That gives traders more flexibility, you can trade when you want to trade, rather than being constrained by the hours kept at the stock market.

The second reason is the size. The size of the Forex market is enormous in comparison to the stock market. On average, $5 trillion per day is traded on the Forex markets. Compare that to just $40 billion per day on the world-famous New York Stock Exchange.

Third, when you trade Forex, you have access to incredible levels of leverage. In some countries it's 100:1, in the United States it's more restrictive, but it's still 50:1. Try to imagine what you could do with stocks using that kind of leverage. Well for stocks, it's not available.

The Forex market is also one of the most liquid trading markets around. That means it's easy to execute your trades. There are a large number of buyers and that makes it easier to get in and out of your positions. Since the market is so liquid, prices change by smaller amounts. Higher liquidity can also mean lower transaction costs.

You can also get started trading Forex with comparatively little capital. To be a day trader of stocks, you need $25,000 cash. To control large amounts of currency on Forex, you can do it with a small amount because of the high leverage. You can get started with as little as $100 or $500, although $1,000 is probably recommended.

Forex also works well with different trading styles and once the veil of mystery is lifted, it's actually pretty simple to understand. In this book, that's what we're going to do. If you're brand new to Forex, you're going to walk away from this book with a solid understanding of what it is and how to go about trading.

Chapter 1: A Quick Overview of Forex

Forex is one of the most exciting trading markets to get involved with, but if you don't know what you're doing, you can quickly find yourself running out of money. In this book, we are going to give you a basic education in Forex from the ground up. Understanding what you're doing and what the limits are is an important part of being successful. To achieve that success, you'll need to have a thorough understanding of how Forex operates, what you can do and the tools of technical analysis used to execute good trades. We're going to teach you all of that in this book.

We'll also see that giving into greed is the downfall of most beginning Forex traders. Having access to massive leverage is a great resource, but it's a double-edged sword – it also gets people into situations where overconfidence and impatience end up getting their accounts closed. We're going to help you avoid that situation with the tools and advice we give in this book.

Why is There a Forex Market and Where Did it Come From?

In order to do international business or travel, people and businesses have to exchange one currency for another. If you're importing goods from a company in Japan, you could pay them in dollars, but at some point, they need to exchange that for their local currency. And in order to make it work right, people, businesses and governments need to know the exchange rates between currencies at any given moment.

Those exchange rates are set by trading on the Forex market. Unlike stock exchanges, there isn't a centralized Forex market and it's lightly regulated. A lot of people are buying and selling different currencies. The value of a currency is set in part by the basic economic principles of supply and demand: if people want more Euros than dollars, the value of the Euro will rise compared to the dollar.

The strength of each country's economy matters too. In the stock market, sometimes we talk about fundamental analysis where you check the fundamentals of a company like its profit margins. For currency, the fundamentals include things like GDP, growth rates, the state of the economy and interest rates. The strength of one currency against another might also depend on political factors. Those things are important if you trade on a long-time window, but many traders trade on short time windows. They can be day traders, or use swing trading techniques in order to make profits.

You're probably coming to Forex expecting to open your own account and start trading. It hasn't always been this way. In fact, the ability of individuals to trade Forex is a relatively recent development. It all started just twenty years ago.

In the old days, the currency exchange used to happen between major banks. This is called *interbank trading.* In short, companies, governments and very high net worth individuals exchanged large amounts of currency through banks in transactions that were settled at the end of each day. Trading was difficult and cumbersome and had high transaction costs. Spreads were wide, making the currency market more illiquid than it should have been. But then, some innovative people changed everything.

Enter the Forex Dealer

In the late 1990s, some people had a brilliant idea. What if they could set themselves up as a middleman and facilitate trades among independent traders? In short, the dealer would trade currency with the bank and then turn around and trade with individual traders. The internet was also booming at the time, so it was easy to set everything up with computers. The FX Dealer was born.

Banks still trade currency with banks and Forex or FX dealers get their liquidity from the banks but pass it on to the trading community. This new setup grew quickly. Within a few years, the popularity of Forex trading was exploding.

The Dealing Desk

When you get down to fundamentals, you can think of an FX Dealer as a broker. When you are trading stocks, a stockbroker or a brokerage plays the role of a middleman. In that case, they run an account for you and when you place orders, they buy and sell stocks for you on a stock exchange and then credit them to your account. Brokers help facilitate trades between people and institutions.

An FX Dealer is essentially doing the same thing. You open an account with an FX Dealer and they facilitate your trades, getting currencies from the banks. There are two types of FX Dealers that you need to be aware of:

- Dealing Desk: A dealing desk is an FX Dealer that will take the other side of your trade so if you want to buy Euros, the dealing desk sells you the Euros directly.
- STP: This means straight-through processing. This type of FX Dealer only plays the role of a middle man and they

don't take the other side of the trade. Instead, what they do is match you up with someone that wants to take the other side of the trade so if you want to buy Euros using dollars, they find someone who has Euros and who wants dollars. That other person might be a bank, but it's not the dealer. It's a third party that wants to take the other side of the trade.

In the early days of Forex, dealing desks were something to be avoided. Since they had their own interests in the trades, they were sketchy. However, today, people aren't concerned with dealing desks and most traders see little difference between STP and Dealing Desks.

If you are a huge trader, there might be some issues. A dealing desk can immediately handle a large trade. An STP might have trouble with this because they would have to find someone to take the other side of the trade who was both capable and interested. By large trade, we're talking 7 or 8 figures so for the vast majority of traders, who are actually small operators, this isn't an issue.

Creating an Account

From here on out we can use the terms "broker" and "FX Dealer" interchangeably. They basically mean the same thing and just like you need to find a broker to trade stocks if you are going to get on the Forex markets, you need a broker to create an account and begin trading.

Opening an account for Forex trading is relatively straightforward, but it's slightly more involved than opening a stock trading account. This is because Forex provides an easy opportunity for money laundering so in order to keep tabs on that, brokers are required to take additional steps to verify your identity. But before you get that far, you'll probably want to know how to select a reputable broker.

The first thing you're going to want to investigate is where the dealer is located. An FX dealer that isn't located in one of the major developed countries might cause you some trouble. If you get into disputes with the broker, you might find customer service difficult or non-existent. And if they owe you money, you might get into a situation where getting your money is problematic. For that reason, you should stick to dealers that are located in countries where there are some regulatory oversight and management by authorities, including regular audits. These countries include the United States, the United Kingdom, Australia and to a lesser extent, Europe. As a hint, you might want to avoid FX Dealers in places like Bermuda or Russia.

Many readers will find it comforting to learn that some familiar names from the stock brokerage world also provide access to Forex trading. This will allow you to set up an account with a company that you already know and trust. After all, connecting your bank account to a dealing desk can, in some cases, be an iffy proposition. For example, TD Ameritrade is a Forex dealer.

When you open your account, you will find that it's pretty like opening an account at a stock brokerage. This is done entirely online, but you will have to fill out an application to open an account. As a part of that application, you'll need to be able to prove you're who you say you are and that you're a resident of the country you are claiming to be living in. As a result, they will require that you submit documentation like a government-issued photo ID and proof of residence, such as a utility bill with your name and address on it.

It will take a couple of days to get your application approved, although some dealers may proceed faster. Once that is taken care of, you can connect your bank account. Again, in order to deal with money laundering issues, you have to fund your Forex account through direct bank wire. You won't be able to use methods like credit cards or PayPal.

Once that is all set up, you are ready to begin trading. All you must do is fund your account and you're ready to go.

Things to Look for in an FX Dealer

The first thing to look for with an FX Dealer is one that provides a wide array of tradable products. Fortunately, that is not an issue when choosing among the leading platforms. Beyond that, you'll want to look for a dealer that has a good user interface that is easy to use and one that has powerful tools available. Charting is the lifeblood of the Forex trader and as we'll see a tool known in the industry as candlesticks is a vital part of that so good charting is a minimal starting point.

You're also going to want access to plenty of research and education tools. This will include a demo or simulated trading account. Why would you want that? The reason is pretty simple: as a beginning trader, it's good to practice first. A demo account lets you execute actual trades in a simulated environment so no real money is used or changing hands, but you can get a feel for it and go through the process of executing trades using the actual exchange rates. This process will help you hone your skills because you can see how your simulated trades work out. Experts often recommend using a demo account for about a month before jumping in with real trades.

In addition to advanced charting capabilities, you'll want a platform that offers plenty of *indicators*. An indicator is a tool that is used to estimate pricing changes in Forex markets some trading platforms offer large numbers of indicators, which can help enhance the odds of trading success.

Spot Market vs. Futures

Our discussion in this book will be about the spot Forex market. The spot market is simply trading one currency against another. One currency is sold and one bought at an agreed exchange rate (the spot exchange rate). The transaction is settled on a specific date called the spot date. Of course, on modern computerized Forex markets, the transaction takes place instantly and so the spot date is the date when you execute the trade.

There is also a futures market for Forex. That isn't a topic that we'll be covering in any detail, but you need to have an awareness that there is such thing. When relevant, we will comment on it.

Chapter 2: Currency Pairs

On stock exchanges, you trade stocks. On Forex, you trade currency, but the currency is always traded in pairs. It would be as if you had to own some stock, but if you were betting on Apple, you had to bet against Microsoft as well. On Forex, currencies are paired one against another such as the Euro against the U.S. Dollar, or the Australian Dollar against the Japanese Yen. Getting familiar with currency pairs and how they are displayed on the Forex markets is the first step in making your way around and understanding what you are doing.

Currency Pair Basics

A currency pair is listed with an abbreviation for the currency some of the most popular currencies include:

- USD: United States Dollar
- EUR: Euro
- JPY: Japanese Yen
- GBP: Great British Pound
- CHF: Swiss Franc
- CAD: Canadian Dollar
- AUD: Australian Dollar
- NZD: New Zealand Dollar

- MXN: Mexican Peso
- RUB: Russian Rubles
- CNY: China Yuan
- SGD: Singapore Dollar

Some currencies also go by nicknames. These include:

- USD: Greenback
- GBP: Cable or Sterling
- AUD: Aussie
- NZD: Kiwi
- CAD: Looney
- EUR: Chunnel
- CHF: Swiss

You should learn what the nicknames of the currencies are or have them referenced so that if you are in discussions about Forex or reading message boards, you have an idea of what people are talking about. If you are wondering where some of these strange names came from, some of them are historical. For example, in the early days of currency trading, undersea cables were used for electronic means of communication between Britain and the United States. That's where the name "cable" came from.

The Majors

Another important concept you need to know about is the *majors*. As you might guess, the majors are the currencies used by the major world economies. However, actually, the majors are expressed in pairs and they represent the most frequently traded currency pairs. The US Dollar is involved in something like 88% of all Forex trades and so more than $4 trillion per day of the currency trading on Forex involves the US Dollar.

The majors are:

- EUR/USD
- USD/JPY
- GBP/USD
- AUD/USD
- USD/CHF
- NZD/USD
- USD/CAD

These seven majors represent 85% of all currency trading. Notice that the United States Dollar is involved in every single one of the major currency pairs. The fact that these pairs represent most of the trading is important because that means that's where you are going to find the most liquidity. That could be significant if you are looking to exit a trade quickly. To complete a trade, you've got to find someone on the other end of it, willing to buy or sell as the case may be.

Many currencies from developing or third world countries are known as "exotics." While the majors are where most of the liquidity is, that doesn't mean you can't profit by trading exotics.

Currency pairs that aren't quoted against US Dollars are called cross-currency pairs. Each currency other than the US Dollar has its own set of cross currency pairs. All currencies trade against one another, but you can consider cross currency pairs just between the majors. For the Euro you have:

- EUR/GBP
- EUR/AUD
- EUR/NZD
- EUR/CAD
- EUR/CHF
- EUR/JPY

Since there are seven majors, all major currencies other than the US Dollar has six cross currency pairs with the other majors.

Currency Pairs Are Expressed in the Same Manner at All Times

You will notice that the currency pairs have one currency that comes first followed by the second currency. These are never changed so, if you are buying Euros and selling dollars, it's EUR/USD and if you are selling Euros and buying dollars, it's still EUR/USD. The first member of a pair is called the *primary* or the *base* currency and the second member of the pair is called the *secondary*, or the *counter* currency. This is just due to historical factors and for labeling purposes, it has nothing do with one currency's relation to the other in the modern world. In centuries past, the GBP was stronger than the US Dollar and so the currency pair has GBP listed first.

Note that on futures markets, the USD is always the secondary or counter currency. That doesn't just mean when the USD is in the currency pair, on the futures markets the USD is always the counter currency so while you'll see USD/JPY on the spot market, you'll see JPY/USD on the futures market. Again, when we are talking about Forex trading in this book, we are talking about the spot market. However, it's important to be aware of what you are looking at in case you happen to come across currency pairs from the futures markets.

Let's run through a few examples.

EUR/USD: The primary is the Euro, the secondary is the US Dollar.

USD/JPY: The primary is the US Dollar; the counter currency is the Japanese Yen.

MXN/JPY: The primary is the Mexican Peso, the secondary (or counter currency) is the Japanese Yen.

The Essence of Currency Pairs

Forex trading boils down to a competition between different currencies. You are trading one against the other and one is going to rise and one is going to fall. When you are using your trading platform, you're going to see listings of currency pairs displayed. EUR/USD is pitting the Euro against the US Dollar and you're betting for one and against the other. Of course, you're not guessing or using "hope," as a Forex trader you're studying the trends and sentiment in the market, using indicators and maybe paying some attention to macroeconomic news in order to make an educated forecast. That doesn't mean it's going to be right of course.

Let's see how this works. Remember that the pairs are always listed in the same order, so you'll have to understand what kind of trade you want to enter in order to pick one currency over the other.

Sticking with EUR/USD, let's say that you believe the Euro is going to rise against the dollar. That means that you're going to want to buy Euros and use your dollars to do it. After that, you hope that when you will sell your Euros, later on, you will get more dollars back than you had originally.

To bet on the Euro for EUR/USD – you are going to *buy* this currency pair. This means you believe the Euro is going to rise and the dollar is going to fall. Remember, everything in Forex is relative. Hence, that means we're saying that the Euro is going to rise compared to the USD. Let's look at some more examples to get some practice with this.

Consider USD/JPY. If you believe that the USD is going to rise and the Japanese Yen is going to fall relative to the dollar, then you will buy this currency pair.

If you believe the Mexican Peso is going to rise relative to the Japanese Yen, then you are going to buy the currency pair MXN/JPY.

Now, remember that the currency pairs are always listed in the same way. Otherwise, if you believe the USD is going to rise against the Euro, how is the transaction going to take place? In that case, you will *sell* the EUR/USD currency pair. Let's say this again:

Selling the EUR/USD currency pair means that you are betting that the USD is going to rise and the Euro is going to fall. When you sell this currency pair, you are selling Euros to buy dollars. Yes, it's confusing, because you probably think that you don't own any Euros. It doesn't matter; the broker/dealer is going to take care of everything for you automatically.

Chapter 3: Pips

The *pip* is a frequently used term in Forex. When you start trading Forex, you're going to have to become intimately familiar with the term pip. In short, pips are the fundamental unit of movement when the value of one currency changes with respect to another. PIP means *percentage in point*. More specifically, one pip is a one-point change in the exchange rate between two currencies.

PIPs are not the smallest unit that you'll see displayed with currency pairs; there is a smaller united that is called a pipette. A pipette is also known as a tick. Most traders don't pay much attention to pipettes.

Quotes and Pips

The first step to getting a handle on pips is understanding how to recognize them. That is, you need to be able to read a quote and identify the pips. For most currency pairs, the pip is the fourth number after the decimal place. Let's run through the pips for some of the majors. In the following, we'll list the quote for each major currency pair and then identify the pip.

- EUR/USD 1.12915: The pip, in this case, is 1. The pipette is 5. Notice that the font size for the pipette is smaller. That's because it's less important (in fact not really important). The font size for the pipette is usually smaller, but not always. We will use both conventions.
- GBP/EUR 1.11523: In this case, which is the Great British Pound and Euro currency pair, the pip is 2.
- AUD/USD 0.69918: For the Australian Dollar/US Dollar pair, the pip is 1.

The Japanese Yen

The Japanese Yen is a unique currency and its fundamental units are 1/100th of other currencies. Therefore, when there is a currency pair involving the Japanese Yen, the pip is located in the second decimal place. The third decimal place is the pipette when the Japanese Yen is a member of a currency pair.

- EUR/JPY 121.490: In this case, the pip is 9. The pipette is 0.
- USD/JPY 107.589: in this case, the pip is 8 and the pipette is 9.

Changes in Currency Pairs

Reading pips from quotes is straightforward enough. When watching currency pair quotes, you're also going to be paying attention to how many pips the exchange rate between the currency pairs has changed. Later, we'll use those to determine profits and losses with trades. Let's use the EUR/USD pair for an example. If it's 1.12915, then it takes $1.13 to buy one Euro.

Suppose that when we look later, the quote is 1.12934. This means that the exchange rate has increased by 2 pips. The pip is now 3 (ignore the pipette). If, instead, the quote was 1.12905, that would mean the exchange rate had decreased by one pip.

Remember, for the Japanese Yen, it's the number in the second decimal place that represents the pip. Therefore, if the USD/JPY quote is 107.589, the pip is 8. If later the quote is 107.558, the exchange rate has dropped by 3 pips. If the exchange rate then goes to 107.569, it's increased by one pip.

Bid/Ask

When you decide you want to enter a trade, currency pairs are quoted in bid and ask terms. If you are selling, the bid value is important, because is the price you'll get by selling the currency pair. To be clear, selling means that you are selling the *base currency pair*. If you are buying a currency pair, the ask price is what you'll have to pay in order to buy the pair. The difference between the bid and ask prices is known as the spread.

If the bid price is quoted at 1.14101 for the EUR/USD pair, it means that if we sell it, 1.14101 is the price that we will receive. If we opt to buy it instead, which would mean we believe the Euro will go up against the dollar, the ask price is the price we must pay to buy Euros. On many trading platforms, the price quotes are listed in the following way:

1.14101/1.14211

The quote is listed as Bid/Ask. On some of the more recent trading platforms, especially in the mobile environment, the straightforward language of Sell and Buy is used instead of Bid and Ask or listing the prices in obscure fashion without explicitly stating what they mean.

Meta Trader 5

Meta Trader 5 (formerly known as Meta Trader 4) is a trading platform. It's a software program that is used to execute Forex trades. It's licensed to a wide range of brokers, so you might use Meta Trader 5 no matter what broker you end up selecting for your trades. You can download it yourself for free, it's also available as an app for the Apple iPhone or Android. If you download the app, you'll have to set it up with your dealer account to execute trades. The app is also useful when pulling up charts and using indicators.

MetaTrader 5

A powerful platform for Forex and Exchange markets

Successful trading on financial markets begins with a comfortable and multi-functional trading platform. MetaTrader 5 is the best choice for the modern trader!

Picture 1

In the screen below, we show a screen from the app displaying a setup for a trade for the EUR/USD pair. On the left side, we see the selling price, if you were selling the pair, which means you expect the Euro to go down, you're going to sell it for

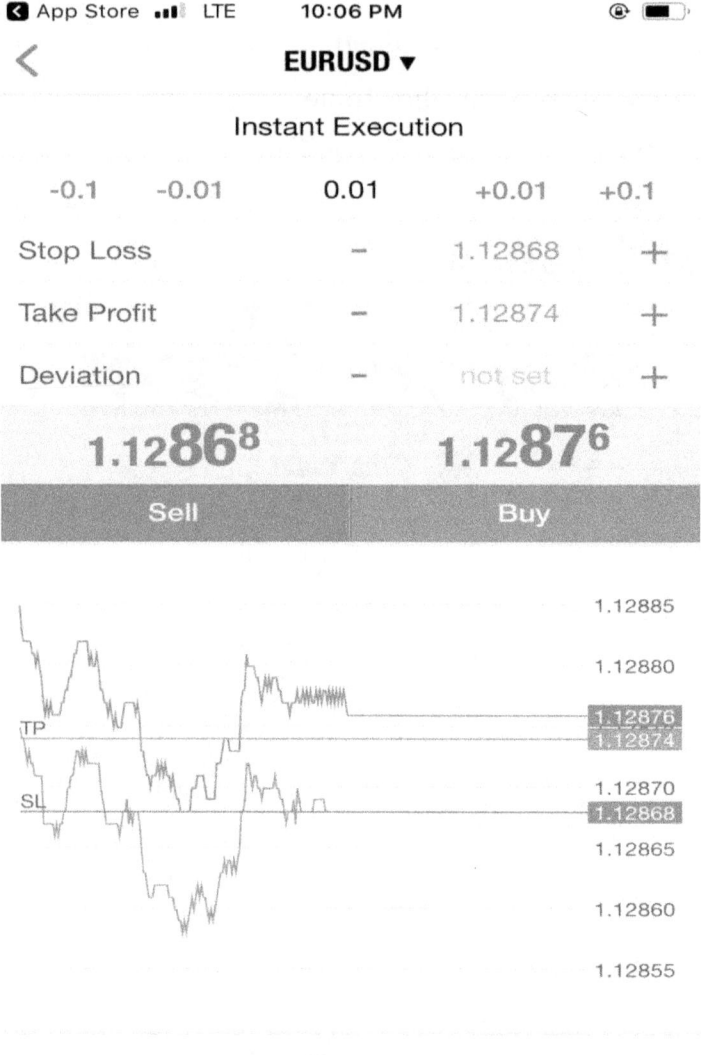

Picture 2

In part, brokers make their profits from the spread in the buying and selling prices. In the screenshot above, the selling price is 1.12868 and the buying price is 1.12876. The difference between the two is 0.00008. The fifth decimal place is the pipette, so the broker would make 8 pipettes, or slightly less than 1 pip, from this transaction. This is a pretty narrow spread. Different brokers will have different spreads and spreads can change at different times. Some brokers offer fixed spreads, but many offer variable spreads. More volatility in an active market can mean wider spreads. While there can be an advantage into trading with fixed spreads, that isn't always the case. Variable spreads can narrow as well.

The spread is your price to enter the trade, then think of it as markup, it's a price that you pay when you enter a trade. Brokers make money from spreads *and* commissions. If you've traded options, you know there is a break-even price. You can think of it this way; your trade is going to have to move at least enough to cover the spread for you to break even.

You'll notice in the screenshot there are a couple of other options. It's important to take note of these and if you are going to be an effective and smart trader, you are going to use them. The first item to note is the *stop loss*. When you enter a trade, you can set a price that you will use to exit the trade if it's going against you automatically. That is the stop loss. You can set this at any value you like; you may want to give yourself a wider room than what the software automatically suggests. The reason you'd do that is that there is always a chance that the price will work against you but reverse at a later time, so you don't want to exit your position prematurely. However, it's smart trading to have a stop loss at some value, so that you won't have your account wiped out by a bad trade.

There is also an option to *take a profit*. This is another automatic trade that you set up to exit the position when the price moves in your favor. You set the take profit price such that you get a preset level of profit and you're satisfied with the trade. Of course, you don't have to do this at any cost; you could manually watch the movements of the currency pair and then manually place your order to exit the trade. However, having a preset "take profit" level enforces discipline. All too often, people become greedy when they see prices rising. That leads them to make bad judgments when they think that prices will continue moving in their favor. You don't want to get into a situation where you're staying in a trade too long with dollar signs in your eyes. All too often, the price will suddenly move against you and you'll end up not making any profit or even losing money. It's better to make a fixed level of profit than it is to walk away with nothing.

Let's make some more examples. Suppose we are trading the USD/JPY pair and the quote is listed as:

107.70/107.73

The left-hand side is the SELL quote. In this case, the spread is 0.03, which is 3 pips. If, instead, the quote was 107.70/107.71, we'd say it had a tighter spread. Since there is less ground to make up, the trader has a higher chance of making a profit. Some brokers will offer tighter spreads, so it's easier for traders to profit. When spreads are tighter, a broker is going to charge a commission. In the world of Forex trading, commissions tend to be small. If the spreads are wider, the broker makes money from the spread and may not charge a commission. You will have to investigate the specifics for the broker that you select.

Entering and Exiting Trades

Remember that if you have a currency pair AAA/BBB, if you sell the currency pair, you are betting that AAA is going to drop in value relative to BBB. If the quote is:

$1.39001/1.39041$

If you sell the currency pair, you start off down 4 pips. If you sell to open the trade, you must buy it back to exit the trade.

If you buy the currency pair, we are betting that AAA is going to increase in value relative to BBB. In this case, you buy to open the position. To close the position, you'll have to sell it.

It's important to realize that you're going to get a debit for the spread no matter what, so it doesn't matter if you buy or sell the currency pair. Here are a couple of examples showing the debits our account would get (in terms of pips) for a couple of different trades.

EURUSD, buy 0.01 1.12885 → 1.12879	-0.06
EURUSD, buy 0.61 1.12888 → 1.12879	-5.49
EURUSD, sell 0.61 1.12879 → 1.12888	-5.49

Picture 3

The point here is notice that if we buy 0.61, you start with a debit of -5.49, if you sell 0.61, you also start with a debit of -5.49. At this point, don't worry about the meaning of the numbers displayed here, simply note that the account gets a debit in both cases.

Depending on what kinds of trades you do, the spread can be more or less important. Some traders attempt to use "scalping," which means that the trader is looking to profit from very small price moves. When scalping, the spread can potentially cut into your profits. If you are doing longer-term trades, then the price moves you are looking to profit from are probably going to be much larger than the spread so that it won't factor very much into your calculations.

Swaps, Interest and Rollover

At 5 PM eastern time in the United States each day, Forex trades that are active are rolled over. This means that the trade is being carried over from one trading day to another. Keep in mind that this happens even though Forex trading is active 24 hours a day. Since the trade is "carried over," a swap is sometimes known as a carry.

Swap is interest. Remember that you're holding money. A swap is an interest you earn (or pay) for each night that the trade is held. Interest is actually paid by the minute, but the numbers are small, so you're not going to get rich holding Forex trades to earn interest on them.

Remember that currency is issued by the central bank in each country. The difference in interest rates between the two countries is what determines what interest you either earn or pay on a trade that you hold overnight. If you are trading the currency pair:

AAA/BBB

If you buy the currency pair, if the interest rate for AAA is higher than the interest rate for BBB, you earn interest. If the interest rate for BBB is higher than the interest rate for AAA, then you would pay interest. If you sell the currency pair, then everything works in reverse. Let's take a look. When selling the currency pair, if the interest rate for AAA is higher than BBB, then you pay interest. But, if you sell the currency pair and BBB has a higher interest rate, then you earn interest.

The swap will be credited or debited as appropriate each evening when the trade is rolled over. Swap is calculated using the following formula:

Swap = (1 point)/(exchange rate)*Trade Size * swap value in points

The swap value in points is the interest rate difference between the two countries in the trade. Note that one point is 0.00001. For the small trades that most individual traders execute, the swap is going to be a trivial amount, it's going to be less than a dollar in most cases, even for very large trades.

Chapter 4: Lots and PIP Value

Before you start trading, you'll have to understand the meaning of all the numbers on your screen and be able to convert pips into actual dollars. We are also going to need to know how currency is traded. It turns out that it has its own world of jargon and specifications. Thus, you can't just say you're going to buy 20 Euros, that is not how it works. There are specific amounts of currency that can be traded. Your broker will determine the amounts you are allowed to trade, based on your account size and leverage. Let's begin by familiarizing ourselves with the way currency is broken down in Forex trading.

Trade Sizes

Trade sizes, also known as *volume*, are specific amounts of currency. These are often described as *units,* but that is just a stand-in for whatever currency you are using. If you are talking about a Great British Pound, the unit is the pound and if you are talking about the US Dollar, the unit is one dollar. Specific values depend on the members of the currency pair, but we will use the EUR/USD pair as a guide. In fact, the values for other pairs will be in a similar range.

There are three trade sizes. These are:

- Micro
- Mini
- Standard

They are also referred to as *lots*. We could say a *standard lot* or *three mini lots*. When Forex trading first became available to individual investors, standard lots were the only option to trade. At that time, they were simply referred to as lots because the other lot sizes had not been devised. As you'll see in a few minutes, it's a good thing that standard lot sizes aren't the only size available, because it involves the control of a large amount of currency.

Micro Lots

A micro lot represents 1,000 units of currency. If it's dollars, a micro is $1,000. A micro is worth 10 cents per pip. The volume or trade size for a micro will be 0.01.

These values are traded in your own currency. We are following the conventions of what an American trader would see. The important thing to know is the cents per pip so that we could frame it the other way – one pip is worth 10 cents. That means that for a micro lot, 10 pips are worth $1.

We want to know the value per pip because you're going to be looking at the quote and looking to see how the number of pips changes in the quote. Then you can move from the numbers of pips to dollars using the value per pip.

Let's see how you could use this information in a practical sense. If the quote for a trade you've bought is 1.23456 and it goes to 1.23486, it's gone up 3 pips. A single micro lot would be worth 30 cents more. On the other hand, if it went up to 1.23686, it's gone up by 0.0023. Therefore, it's up by 23 pips. That means the trade has increased in value by $2.30.

If you were to trade 5 micro lots, the value per pip would be $0.50. In order to trade five micro lots, the volume or trading size would be 0.05.

It's important to practice a lot of calculations like this so that it becomes second nature.

Mini Lots

A mini lot is ten times larger than a micro lot. Since it's ten times larger, the volume or trade size of a mini lot is 0.10. This means that you are trading 10,000 units of currency, or expressed in terms of U.S. dollars, you're trading $10,000 with a mini lot. If you are trading 2 mini lots, then it's $20,000.

For a mini lot, the relationship with pip is $1 per pip or 1 pip per $1. A 10 pip move on a mini lot is a $10 move in price. If you trade five mini lots, then the value per pip is $5 and a 10-pip move would be a change in price by $50. These numbers seem small, but, as you'll find out, they can add up to big numbers real quick.

Standard Lots

The standard lot is the largest possible lot, thank God we have to stop somewhere. A standard lot is 100,000 units of currency. If you are talking about dollars, this means that you're talking about trading $100,000 for each standard lot., ten standard lots would be a cool million dollars.

In the case of a standard lot, the volume or trade size is 1.0. To trade three standard lots, volume or trade size would be 3.0.

The value per pip, in this case, is $10, then, if you make 10 pips on a trade, that means you've made $100.

What Kinds of Trades Can You Make

In the next chapter, we'll see that with Forex, you have a large amount of leverage available. As we mentioned earlier, that can be a double-edged sword. High amounts of leverage can help people get into trades and hence earn profits that they otherwise couldn't do. The downside of this is that you don't always win at trading. And when you lose, leverage can cause some people to wipe out their accounts. In Forex, they will close your trades and then shut down your account if it gets out of control. I am sure that this is not something you're going to want to happen, so you should start small no matter how much money you plan to put into Forex. Learn to trade first and stick with small trades, so that if your trades go back, you can live for another Forex trading day, rather than leaving humiliated and having your account shut down.

For beginning traders, trading micro lots is the best way to proceed. In fact, Forex dealers often have specialized accounts for small traders called micro accounts. To open a micro account, you're going to deposit $1,000 or less in order to open the account. To get anywhere, you'll probably want to deposit $1,000, but if you only have a small amount of money to start with, that's a fair thing to do. That way, you can get started trading and hopefully build up your account from the inside if you get some profitable trades. Remember to think safely and play small, don't get into Forex trading hoping to make a million dollars right off the bat.

To get an idea of what can happen, you should note that large moves can happen very quickly on Forex. A 100 pip move in a matter of seconds isn't unheard of. For a micro lot, there are 10 pips per dollar. A 1% move in the price of a currency can wipe out your entire account.

In order to trade mini lot sizes, you will probably have to have at least $5,000 in your account. Remember that a mini lot is 10 times the size of a micro lot.
Finally, if you are looking to trade standard lots, you should open an account with at least $20,000.

However, even if you can trade standard lots – we don't recommend it. Trading small and using stop-loss orders is the best way to protect your account from massive losses.

Chapter 5: Margin and Leverage

One of the most powerful tools a trader can have is a margin account. This provides leverage, that is the ability to trade quantities that are much larger than you could afford using your own cash. On the stock market, you need $2,000 in order to open a margin account and you're able to get a 2:1 margin. That means with $2,000 you can buy $4,000 worth of stock.

Forex has amazing leverage and that's one of the reasons that it has attracted so many traders. In the United States, there is 50:1 leverage available to Forex traders. That means if you had $1 in cash, you could trade $50 worth. If you had a $1,000 account, you would have the ability to trade $50,000. Other countries have more flexible leverage. The United Kingdom, Europe and Australia allow 100:1 leverage, so in that case, you could trade $100,000 with a $1,000 account. However, it's expected that over time, everyone is going to adopt the 50:1 standard. Even if they do, keep in mind that is quite generous.

When thinking about leverage, it's a good idea to remember the amounts of currency that you control with each lot size. To review:

- Micro lot: With a micro lot size, you would control $1,000 in currency.
- Mini lot: With a mini lot size, it's ten times as large. That means you control $10,000 in currency.
- Standard lot: Once again, it's a tenfold increase in the amount you control, then a standard lot is $100,000.

Whenever you look at your margin and leverage, you'll want to keep in mind the lot size and how much you could control if you used all your leverage. That said, we don't recommend using all your leverage. You can be sure of trade and it's not going to work out. It's as necessary to think about losing trades as it is to think about winning trades.

What is Margin

In Forex, the margin is a "down payment" that you make on a trade. It's the percentage of the trade that you must put up in cash. You can think of leverage as a loan and, in short, that's what it is. The broker is lending you the cash that you would need in order to execute a given trade.

Sometimes margin is expressed as a percentage: in the United States it's 2%, that would mean that the minimum percentage you'd have to put up in cash to execute any trade is 2%. You can use the percentage to determine how much in absolute amounts of currency you can trade by diving your account size by 2%, which means you divide it by 0.02. Here are some examples of how much we could control, at least in theory, for a few different small account sizes:

- $500 – you could control $25,000
- $1,000 – you could control $50,000
- $2,500 – you could control $125,000
- $5,000 – you could control $250,000
- $10,000 – you could control $500,000

These are astounding numbers! This is the kind of thing that gets new Forex traders excited. With a small amount of money, you can control amounts of currency that you've probably never dreamed of.

Looking at Lots

Remember that trading is done in lots. You have to specify whether it's a micro, mini, or standard lot and then specify how many lots are in the trade. It's good practice to look at using a certain dollar amount that you're willing to commit to a trade and then figuring out how much cash that translates into using leverage. Then, from there, figure out how many lots of what type you could trade.

Let's start by looking at some small dollar amounts. Suppose that you were able to commit $100 to a trade, if you divide by 0.02, you get $5,000.

Now, remember that a micro lot is $1,000, therefore, if you put up $100 on a trade, that means that you'll be able to trade 5 micro lots. Since a mini lot is $10,000, you can't trade a mini lot.

Now suppose that you put up $500, instead. When we did our calculations above, we found out that using $500 we could have the ability to access to $25,000 using leverage. That's astonishing when you think about it. We've only increased the amount of money that we are putting down for the trade by $400, but that increased the amount we can trade by $20,000.

With $25,000, we could trade 2 mini lots or 25 micro lots. Unfortunately, you can only trade the whole number values of lots so you can't trade 2.5 mini lots, you can trade 2 mini lots or 3 mini lots. To use up the entire amount of leverage, we'd have to go with the micro lots.

When entering your trades, you want to figure out the dollars per pip. That way, you'll be able to quickly determine the number of dollars you've made or lost when the exchange rate changes by a given number of pips.

If you are trading 5 micro lots, we recall that for a micro lot there is a relationship of 10 pips per $1, which is ten cents per pip. A five micro lot trade would mean that a 1 pip move would be a 50-cent change in price. A 150 pip move would amount to a $75 change in price. That can either be a gain or loss – don't forget.

In the case of the $25,000 trade, that's 25 micro lots, a 1 pip move would be a $2.50 change in price. A 100 pip move would be $250 and a 150 pip move would be $375.
When you enter a trade, the broker will take the margin out of your account. Consequently, if you enter a trade using $500 cash with 50:1 leverage, you can make a $25,000 trade and they are going to deduct $500 from your account balance.

Although this is just simple arithmetic, you should keep practicing and try different numbers so that you can look at trades and know what they entail quickly.

Another way to look at things is to do your calculations in the other direction. That is: imagine how many lots of different sizes you'd like to buy and then work backward to find out how much cash you need to put up.

Let's say that you wanted to trade 7 mini lots. That's 70,000 units of currency and the trading volume would be 0.70. How much cash do you need? You simply take $70,000 x 2% = $1,400.

Standard lots are the province of the big traders, generally speaking. Maybe you could put up enough cash to trade standard lots, but you'll have to ask yourself if the potential losses are worth it.

For example: you want to trade five standard lots. Each standard lot is 100,000 units of currency, so if we trade five lots, that means we're looking at $500,000. You can just multiply by the percentage or divide by the leverage and using the latter we get $500,000/50 = $10,000. That means that with the aim of making the trade to control 500,000 units of currency, we need $10,000 cash.

Remember that formula:

Currency units/Leverage = down payment required

In the United States, leverage is 50:1, so the formula is:

Currency units/50 = down payment required

In the UK, Australia and Europe, you can use 100:1 and so the formula would be:

Currency units/100 = down payment required

To trade 5 mini lots in the United States, which would be 50,000 currency units, we need:

$50,000/50 = $1,000

Ergo, we could enter the trade if we can put up $1,000 cash.

Account Info

Your Forex trading platform is going to have everything summarized for you, showing you the values of different quantities. These include:

- Balance: The amount of cash in your account to start. That is before you enter any trades.
- Equity: This will be your balance, plus or minus your open trades.
- Margin: The total amount of margin currently used on trades.

- Free Margin: The actual amount of margin available, that is margin – used margin.
- Margin Level: This is the ratio of free margin to margin expressed as a percentage so if my free margin is $9,800 and my margin is $5,000, my margin level is 9800/5000 x 100 = 196%. This gives you an idea of how much margin you have left to make trades. Over 100% is good.
- Useable margin: This will be Equity – Margin.

If you have no open trades, then equity is simply equal to the balance. Free margin is the margin that is available to make more trades. If you have free margin available and you enter a losing trade, free margin can be used to cover it. However, remember that this means less margin available for future trades.

Margin Call

If there is one phrase that is a leading candidate for most dreaded words in the human language for traders, it's *margin call*. This is when you must deposit enough cash into your account to bring your account back into good standing, or the broker can close your positions and your account.

If Equity is larger than used margin, then there won't be a margin call. If equity is less than or equal to used margin, there will be a margin call.

Let's say we start with an account with $5,000. The total amount we can trade would be $250,000. The margin required would be $100.

To determine how many pips a trade would have to move in order to get a margin call, you need to know your dollars per pip and the dollar amount of usable margin. A mini lot is $1 per pip and there are 10,000 currency units. In order to trade 9 mini lots with 50:1 margin, we need $1,800 cash, which is the amount of margin required. With a trade of nine lots, we are at $9 per pip. Less $1,800 cash, we are left with a $3,200 for the cash portion of our equity. Your cash left over is your usable margin. At $9/pip, to get a margin call your trade would have to drop $3200/$9 = 355 pips. It's certainly possible for it to drop that much.

At this point, used margin is $1,800 and usable margin has dropped to $3,200. That means we can enter another trade where the total is $160,000 or less.

Let's say we enter another trade, using $3,000 margin. That gives us $150,000 in buying power, therefore, we can buy 15 more mini lots. We are now long 24 mini lots. Our used margin is $4,800 and if the equity falls below the usable margin value, which is now only $200, there would be a margin call. To find out how many pips our position would have to drop by for this to happen, let's do some calculations. A mini is $1/pip.

We have $1/pip x 24 lots = $24/pip

That means if the currency pair goes up by 1 pip, equity increases by $24. If it goes down by 1 pip, equity decreases by $24. And now we only have $200 in usable margin. The room we have is $200/$24 = 8 pips. A slight change in the currency value would eat up our account. It's quite possible that the broker would close out the trade automatically to keep us from getting into too much trouble.

When you get a margin call, your trade is closed at the current market price. That means you're stuck with the loss.

Chapter 6: Influencers of the Forex Markets

Any financial market is influenced by a wide array of factors. On the stock market, company news can drive an individual stock to new heights or make it since to new lows. A good jobs report can send the S & P 500 soaring, which means that most companies are going to see their stock rising. A trade deal gone bad can send things in the other direction.

What influences the Forex market? Many things can drive prices one way or another. Anything from a trade war to a shooting war to simple supply and demand can help drive action on the Forex market. At the center of it all are the individual traders, who are driving prices up and down with their own desires to make money and fear of losing it all. Let's have a look at all the players on the market that influence Forex.

Market Makers

If you remember, at the beginning of the book, we discussed how Forex trading used to take place primarily between banks. A lot of Forex trading still goes on between banks. In the business, this is known as the interbank Forex market. It's done by computer now, but this is the same kind of trading that went on between the banks before the advent of the retail trading market created by the FX dealers. Market makers influence the Forex markets through interbank trading.

Every bank has a market maker. In fact, they have a market maker for all the majors. Hence, at the very least, the bank will have seven market makers, with each market major managing one of the major currency pairs. The job of the market maker is to set a price that the bank is willing to pay at the time for a given currency pair. Since banks deal with an enormous amount of currency compared to retail traders, any move made by a bank is going to have a huge influence on the exchange rates. Through the market maker, they set the parameters for each of the major currency pairs. These are the market makers, in the truest sense of the word.

Of course, competition between banks helps dampen the impact. Different banks throughout the world have their own market makers and they will have their own buying and selling terms and they will have to meet in the middle in order to come to terms.

Each market maker operates from a starting point of bid and ask prices for their currency pair. They can make deals with other big players. Banks can do currency trading using credit terms, which magnifies the impact of their deals because they are much larger than they would be in cash.

Market makers can also be hedge funds or broker-dealers. These people set the rates on the retail markets where individual traders trade. While this sounds bad at first, it shouldn't put you off as far as entering trades. The reason is that there is not one market marker on the retail market. There are many market makers – remember that any FX dealer acts as a market maker. On the retail market, the market makers know they can attract more traders by having the best deals. This generates competition among the market makers, which can help individual traders get better deals.

One of the most important ways that the market makers help individual traders is by maintaining liquidity in the markets. That is, they ensure that when you want to enter a trade, you're able to do so and do it instantly. Moreover, broker-dealers acting as market makers can offer more favorable spreads, which means lower costs for you to enter the trade.

You might be asking at this point how do the banks play a role here. Remember that the broker-dealers have to trade with the banks. It's important to keep the complete picture of the Forex market in your head. While the broker-dealers can trade directly with individual traders, or facilitate trading between individual traders, behind it, all the brokers are trading with the banks. That means the banks have a fundamental influence on what's going on. In other words, the banks are influencing things by the exchange rates that they are willing to accept in deals and so they influence the starting point for the brokers. That is going to set constraints on what the spreads are as well.

Political Factors and Foreign Affairs

There are so many factors that can influence the strength of currency; it's hard even to list them all. One thing that has always influenced currency prices relative to one another is the international situation. Since the end of World War Two, or even before, the dollar has been seen as the go-to international currency. People view the United States government as strong and immovable. Whether or not that is still justified is an open question, but that has been the perception and it continues in the present, at least for now.

A consequence of this is that if there is international trouble, people are going to look to move their money into dollars. One thing that is true all around the world is that people will accept dollars as payment. Do you see people clamoring in order to get their hands-on Chinese currency? Of course not. Who would want it? China might dream of a world where they have the reserve currency, but the reality is even now that's not anywhere near happening. The Chinese government is a totalitarian state and people don't trust them. That isn't to say the United States government is peaches and cream. That isn't the point – but the U.S. economy remains the largest and most stable in the world. The fact that China's currency isn't contained in any major trading pairs should tell you something.

If there is a war, then people will be moving their currency into U.S. dollars fast. God forbid, if a war happens during a time when you are Forex trader, you'd be smart to move to favor the US dollar in your trades. Now let's be clear, we are talking about a major war where everyone's security is threatened, not some kind of "police action" like an invasion of Iraq. The United States doesn't have to be involved at all to cause a significant strengthening of the U.S. dollar. In recent years, China has been getting into lots of territorial disputes with its neighbors. Suppose for a moment that this turned into a "hot" war. A lot of friendly countries are in the area, including Australia, Japan and South Korea. They'd all feel very threatened, the dollar would immediately become stronger, as currency traders would be bidding up the price of dollars on the Forex markets.

Speaking of South Korea, that is something to watch as well. The North Koreans have settled down lately, but anything that leads to instability in the Pacific region or Europe bodes well for the US Dollar.

Inflation Rates

When you have low inflation rates, it helps your currency. Maybe to get a grip on this we can think about what doesn't help your currency. If you have really high inflation, it means it takes a lot more currency to buy the same goods than it took in the past. When inflation rates are high, the time periods over which money becomes worthless can be surprisingly short. While developed countries are more stable, high inflation rates can happen. In the late 1970s inflation rates in the United States skyrocketed. They weren't at Zimbabwe levels, but at 13-14% they made life in the US far more difficult than it would have been otherwise. Everyone also recalls that in the 1920s, Germany experienced out of control inflation. It was so bad that people had to use wheel barrels to carry huge amounts of cash around just to buy basic staples like coffee or a loaf of bread. Too bad credit cards hadn't been invented yet.

A high rate of inflation definitely weakens the value of a currency, but the real factor is the comparison of inflation rates between countries that are in a currency pair. If Europe had a 1% inflation rate, but Canada had a 10% inflation rate, that would favor the

Euro over the Canadian dollar in currency trading, all other things being equal. Remember that a 10% inflation rate means that the purchasing power of the Canadian dollar would be dropping 10% a year so if you could buy 10 apples last year using one Canadian dollar, this year you could only buy nine. And if you don't have as much purchasing power at home, you'd expect to buy less with Canadian dollars anywhere, which means you could also buy fewer Euros with them as well. Of course, some of this is just common sense, if Canada had high inflation, individual traders and banks around the world would be shying away from their desire to own Canadian dollars.

Interest Rates

The interest rates set by the central banks throughout the world can have an impact on the strength of currency as well. This can be related to inflation since central banks will raise interest rates in order to try and tamp down inflation. This also happened in the United States in the late 1970s, when the US Federal Reserve began raising interest rates to try and get inflation under control. Interest rates went as high as 18%, causing the media to create the "misery index."

But like inflation, when comparing two countries, it's the differences in interest rates that matter. Higher interest rates can help a country's currency strengthen. The reason for this is simple. People are always looking for a return on their money, that is they want to make more money than they presently have. When interest rates are high, this can provide a lot of opportunities to make money while preserving capital at the same time. Therefore, if interest rates are higher in one country relative to another, it's going to attract investment dollars – that is foreign capital will start flowing into the country so that they can invest in anything that generates interest payments. It could be investing in bonds, real estate, or any asset that will result in interest payments. But guess what, if you want to invest in country AAA, you must convert your currency into the currency AAA. That's a higher demand for AAA, which means its value is going to rise relative to the country that is the source of the funds. If the United States had high-interest rates, but Europe kept theirs artificially low, then money would flow from Europe to the United States to take advantage of the high-interest rates and this would drive up the value of the US dollar relative to the Euro.

Rising Government Debts

A high and rising government debt can weaken a currency over time. This happens because foreign investors are less interested in investing in a country that carries a large amount of debt. Government debt has an impact that can be said to "crowd out" investment. Again, everything is relative. The United States has let its debt get out of control over the past 10 years, so you would think that would be a negative. Maybe the Japanese Yen would end up being stronger relative to the dollar. However, Japan has let its government debt get out of control too so it's hard to see who has a favorable position relative to this one data point.

International Trade

A country that is importing a lot of goods can weaken its currency. If AAA is importing a lot of goods from BBB, that means BBB has to accept large amounts of payments in AAA currency, which they are going to have to sell in order to get their own currency back, or companies in AAA will trade for BBB currency in order to buy the goods with BBB currency. In either case, the importer is the loser in this situation, since there will be a routine sell-off of the AAA currency as they continue importing more goods.

Economic Strength

The overall strength of the economy can be a huge factor, as well. If a company has low unemployment, is creating jobs and GDP growth is strong, then this can strengthen its currency relative to competitors.

Fears and Hopes of Individual Traders

Individual traders can help strengthen a trend in the markets caused by other forces. The reason is that people tend to engage in herd behavior. When traders start seeing a rising US dollar relative to the Euro, they are going to try and jump on the trend, which is only going to act to strengthen it even more. The same goes if they see a weakening dollar, then individual traders will be betting against the dollar, in the hopes of earning profits.

The Bottom Line

Many factors influenced the Forex markets. In each case, it's important to remember that everything is relative. In other words, what's important is not really the absolute value of any metric that we discussed here. The relative value between trading countries is what matters. In each case, you should take the difference in whatever quantity you are interested in for two trading countries to determine if that favors one country or another. If Mexico has 8% inflation, in the United States has 2% inflation that obviously favors the United States.

In the next chapter, we are going to return to our direct discussion on Forex. We are going to give a qualitative overview of the strategies used by Forex traders.

Chapter 7: An Overview of Forex Trading Strategies

In this chapter, we are going to discuss the strategies used by Forex traders. The discussion in this chapter is going to be of a qualitative nature. In later chapters, we are going to dive more into the specific tools that are used by Forex traders. Those tools involve chart analysis and technical indicators. Those are important, but it's also important to understand the overall strategies and approaches used by traders.

Everyone has their own trading style. Everyone also has their own favorites among all the tools are used in order to try and get favorable trades. As a new trader, you're going to find this a little bit overwhelming. The key for a new trader is to sample different tools and find the ones that fit their personality and abilities best. For example, if it's true that technical analysis gives certain traders an edge, but you aren't inclined to use technical analysis that really doesn't make it an edge for you. In other words, you may not be so good at using technical analysis in order to help your trades., in that case, it might be better to look for other approaches.

Candlesticks

Candlesticks and trading bars are related tools that many traders use. They both contain the same information, but candlesticks are by far the most popular. We are going to spend an entire chapter talking about candlesticks, but, right now, we are just going to give you an overview that discusses the information provided by candlesticks and what they're used for.

The first thing to know about candlesticks is that they tell you the open and closing price for a given trading period. By trading period, we mean different ranges of time. You could divide up your charts into one-minute intervals, or you could use four-hour intervals or even one-day intervals., if you were using four-hour intervals, that would mean that the candlestick provided the opening price at the beginning of the four-hour period and the closing price at the end of the four-hour time period. The time frame that you would use will depend on the preferences that you take when making your trades.

Candlesticks also tell you whether prices were rising or falling over the timeframe. This is usually indicated by color, with green candlesticks representing rising prices and red candlesticks indicating falling prices. Since you can either buy or sell a currency pair, the meaning and importance of the color are significant, depending on the position that you've taken. On many charts, different color schemes can be used. Normally, when colors are used to represent rising prices, are indicated with a hollow candle body. A white or black solid body would be used to represent a candlestick with the following price.

Candlesticks also have wicks that are sticking out of the candlestick body. Unlike a real candlestick, the candlesticks used on financial charts have wicks that stick out both from the bottom and the top. With these, candlesticks tell you which are the high and low prices for the time frame. As we will find out in a later chapter, various patterns that are seen on charts with candlesticks can indicate a trend in one direction or another.

The strategy with candlesticks is to utilize the patterns seen on the chart in order to determine upcoming trends. When the trader sees a pattern that indicates a rising price, then, they can enter a trade to bet for the currency pair. On the other hand, if they wanted to sell, they could be looking for signals of a calming drop in price.

The truth is almost every Forex trader uses candlesticks in their analysis., even if you don't use them extensively, it's something that you're going to want to understand.

Fundamental Analysis

Many traders or investors have heard about fundamental analysis when it comes to the stock market. In that case, it means looking at the fundamentals of an individual company, such as determining whether they are positioned to continue making profits. Of course, in Forex, we don't have any individual companies. That said, there's plenty of room to do fundamental analysis. In this case, you're going to be looking at macroeconomic factors, political factors, interest rate risk and international trade. The overall health and state of the country's economy and political situation are going to have a big impact on the value of its currency.

In the present environment in the United States, for example, interest rates are far less of a factor than they have been historically. That being said, if you've been following the news, you'll realize that the Federal Reserve has been a little bit anxious to raise rates, hence, there may be interest rate increases coming. Even if interest rates are not particularly important right now, they may be important in the future. This could be in the near-term future over the next couple of years.

That was about some macroeconomic news that can all have an influence on the strength of the currency. One of the first things that are important is consumer spending. Employment is also important and GDP growth rates are going to have a huge influence on the strength of an economy and the perception of its strength. Actually, I should say that GDP growth reflects the strength of an economy and it's certainly going to drive the strength of the currency. Again, relative comparisons are what matter the most., in other words, if the United States is growing at 4% GDP growth and Europe is also growing at 4%, that won't have much of an impact. However, if the United States is growing up 4% GDP growth and Europe is growing at 1% GDP growth or even 2%, we'll have a large impact weakening the euro and strengthening the dollar. The high GDP growth rate in the United States is going to be attractive to big investors in Europe. They are going to want to move some other capital into the United States. It will also attract investors from other parts of the world who will choose to invest in the United States rather than in Europe. As far as the Forex market is concerned, this means that the demand for dollars will increase. Whenever an investor from a foreign country enters the United States, they are going to have to change their currency into dollars.

The housing market is also another important indicator of the health of the economy. Even though it won't be a priority, it's something that you should be checking in the background.

Jobs reports can have a big impact at least in the short-term. One thing you will notice is that when there is a good job report, the

69

stock market will skyrocket. Of course, the opposite can happen as well. The key point here is that anything that makes an economy look dynamic, healthy and growing is going to attract investment from elsewhere and help grow the economy.

Of course, there are many important macroeconomic indicators that we discussed as influencers in the past chapter. These are all important when doing fundamental analysis. Any trader that uses fundamental analysis as part of their strategy is going to pick a currency pair. Then, they will do an analysis of these factors for each country in the currency pair. After that, they can get relative differences, such as the relative difference in the inflation rates of the countries. Traders that are looking over long-term horizons will find this kind of information more important. By making relative comparisons, the trader can estimate which economy's going to be stronger in the coming weeks or months. The bet here would be which direction currency would flow, as a result, the trader can either bet for or against the currency pair based on this information.

Scalping

Many Forex traders use a technique called scalping. This involves entering a position for a very short period of time, hoping to make profits from short-term price movements. The profit from any single trade will be small. A Forex trader that is using scalping makes up for the small profits per trade by doing lots of trades. The games that traders are looking for fall in the range of 5 pips up to about 20 pips. You can go back to the earlier chapters and then see for different lot sizes what kind of profit that would be.

The profits obtained from a single trade is actually very small. This puts the scalper in the position of having to enter lots of trades, but there are trade-offs to be made. One of the trade-offs is that scalpers tend to trade small. And what that means, is that they have low risk per trade as well.

If you have a larger account and can risk more money on a trade, then you can make tens of dollars in profit off the very small move in currency price. Putting $10,000 on the trade - depending on the kind of move you would be looking for, could possibly net you a couple of hundred dollars in profit. Since the movements they are looking for are small, they don't have to stay in their trades very long. This could make it possible to do multiple trades per day. One of the advantages would be that a trader could actually make a full time living by doing multiple trades every single day.

Scalpers sometimes have to use electronic communication networks or ECNs to be successful. This helps them get more liquidity and can help them connect with larger market players.

One of the biggest problems with scalping is that you must be concerned when you were taking small levels of profit, that it's not going to be enough to overcome the spread. Remember that any time you enter a Forex trade, you start out with a negative balance as a result of the spread. You need to overcome that just breakeven. If you're talking about very small moves on the order of 5-20 pips, overcoming the expense of the spread might be difficult.

Swing Trading

Swing trading is a totally different approach. In this approach, the trader seeks to find big swings in market prices., let's imagine that we are hoping the price of a currency pair will rise. The swing trader will look for zones of support and resistance that define the range over which the currency pair normally trades. Then, the swing trader will wait until the currency pair price drops near the zone of support, which serves as a barrier for the lowest possible price of the currency pair. When the price moves to this point, that is the ideal entry point for the trade. When the swing trader enters a trade, they will patiently wait for the price to rise to a level over which they want to take profits. A swing trader is willing to hold their trades over an extended time. This is not a long-term trade, in the sense that they would keep their trade for a year or something like that. However, swing traders are willing to keep the position for several days, weeks and even out to a couple of months.

Swing traders will be entering fewer trades than scalpers. That's because they're looking for big swings in market prices. The sizes of profits available to them, when they make a winning trade, are going to be higher relatively to the one obtained by a scalper.

One thing that we can say that all traders have in common is that all traders are tempted to trade the trend. This means that you will look for trends in one direction or another. Then what you do, as you jump on the trend, and write it to the inevitable position where you can exit and take your profits.

Position Trading

Position trading as a strategy is something that can be said to be an extension of swing trading. This is a long-term approach where you can stay in your trades for even months at a time. In this case, the trader will use fundamental analysis. That's because, over the long-term, the factors considered in fundamental analysis become more important., for example, the longer you hold a currency pair, the more important become the economic trends in the two countries. Also, there might be certain events, such as one country might raise its interest rates, so that they are higher relative to the other country. The longer that you hold a trade, the more important these types of events become.

That isn't to say that other types of analysis are not important for position traders. Position traders will use tools like candlesticks, too. That will be important to tell them when to enter a trade and when to exit a trade. Like swing traders, they will use support and resistance to help them make their decisions.

Day Trading

You've probably heard about day traders on the stock market, but there are also day traders on Forex. Day trading is basically like swing trading but using short-term time frames. A day trader attempts to get in and out of the trade during the same trading day. Trades can be held for hours, but they can also be held for short periods that last between five and 20 minutes. It's not quite scalping, because the day trader may seek to earn a much higher profit then a scalper would., like swing traders, a day trader would probably enter a trade at a level of support. Then, they would exit their trade at resistance. They also look for phenomena such as breakouts, which are sudden breaks to an upward or downward trend. Day traders are not going to be concerned about things like fundamental analysis. You can't say that they won't be concerned at all, because there could be something like an announcement of an interest rate change that could drive the markets, but on most days, day traders are operating on a short time skill; therefore it's unlikely that such things are going to impact their trades.

Retracements

Consider a trend that is strong in one direction or another. When any financial assets are trading in the trend, you're going to see a lot of wavy lines up-and-down. In other words, the trend is not going up in a straight line and there are times when the price drops back - appearing to reverse. But then you see the price resume it's inevitable climb or descent.

These kinds of moves are known as *retracements*. A retracement provides a trader with an opportunity to get in on the trend. The way that you take advantage of this is to wait for the price to move to a low point (if we are considering going long) and that's when you enter your trade. Then you wait for the trend to resume and take your profits at the appropriate level.

Trading a Market

One strategy that some traders use is looking for trends that occurs slightly before one market closes and another opens., for example, a trader could attempt to find a currency pair that was in a strong trend just before market close in the United States. The goal here would be to get in on the trend before it takes off as New York closes and London opens. In the financial markets, there are often strong moves which take place within the first 30 minutes when the market opens. Since Forex operates 24 hours a day, you could benefit by holding your positions after the market closes and then riding the uptrend when the next market opens.

Currency Pairs

Calling this one strategy currency pairs might seem a little facetious. Obviously, every Forex trade is a currency pair. But what we are talking about in this strategy is forgetting about focusing so much on the majors. All too many traders simply want to trade any currency against the US dollar. But that misses the point because the essence of trading - it is to get more money out of it then you started with. The members of the pair aren't really that relevant. The thing that is relevant is by how much the pairs are moving. There are software tools that you can use to help you pick out pairs that are showing strong movement in one direction or another. That way, you can get in on trades where are the big movements in price. This can help you earn larger profits. The only problem with this strategy is avoiding currency pairs that have low liquidity.

Chapter 8: Candlesticks

Candlesticks are one of the most important tools used by Forex traders. They help determine recent market sentiment by telling us the price movement of a recent period. Understanding candlesticks will be important for your success as a Forex trader, helping you forecast future price moves by observing certain well-known patterns. Luckily candlesticks aren't very complicated.

Candlestick Basics

A candlestick represents price changes for a given time period. The graphic below shows how to understand candlesticks.

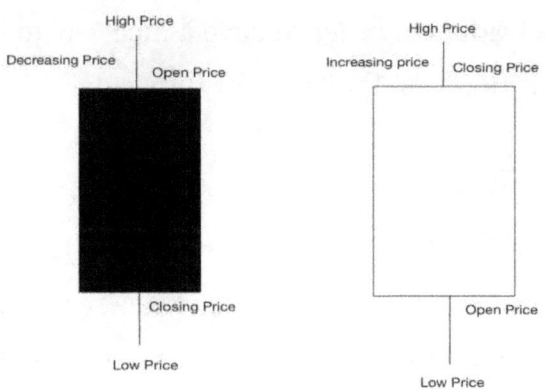

Picture 4

On the left, the solid black candlestick represents a price decline for the period the candlestick represents, which can be anything from 1 minute to a day or even a week or year. You can select the time frame you want to use on your charts provided by the trading platform. The candlestick on the right side, which has a hollow body, is representative of a price increase. Several color schemes can be used. The most popular is green for the price increase and red for a price decrease. Many traders like to use charts with black backgrounds and sometimes these have the colored candlesticks, which use red for price decrease and green for the price increase, or they use white for a price decrease and a hollow body outlined in white for a price increase.

There are also bars available that provide the same information that candlesticks do, but it's just a different shaped object. Most traders use candlesticks. These were originally developed in Japan by rice traders in order to have a nice way to keep track of price changes and make forecasts for future developments.

You will notice that there are lines sticking out of the candlestick. These are usually called wicks but are also called shadows. The end of the top wick represents the high price reached for the time period. The end of the bottom wick represents the low price for the period. Opening and closing prices are represented by the body, but there are different meanings depending on the type of candlestick. For a decreasing price, the top of the body represents the opening price. The closing price is given by the bottom of the body. If you think about it, this makes sense, because the opening price will be lower than the closing price if prices dropped for the given period.

For a price increasing candlestick, which is either hollow or green, the opening price is given by the bottom of the candlestick while the top of the body gives the closing price.

The length of the body will tell you if there was a lot of price movement from opening to the closing. On the left in the next image, we have a candlestick that had a closing price far above the opening price. A high closing price could be a good sign for the next upcoming time period since buyers of the currency pair were entering trades and pushed the price up high.

The candlestick on the right shows a different situation. In this case, the price was pushed up high during the day, but it also went quite a bit lower than the opening price. The narrow body tells us that despite this price movement, the closing price only narrowly exceeded the opening price.

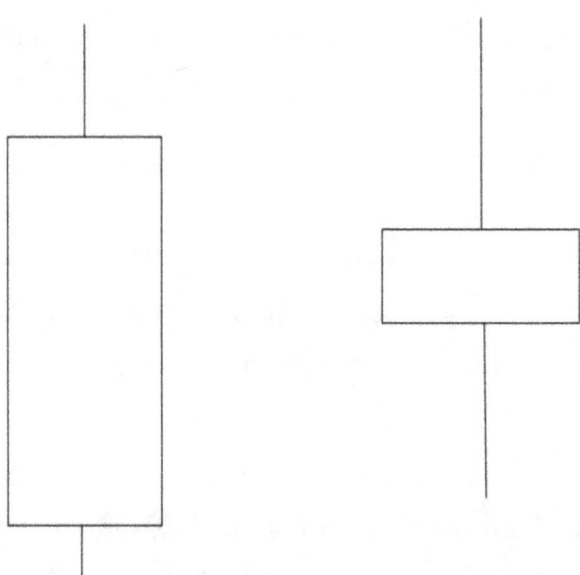

Picture 5

Also, note that the wicks can be of different lengths. Some candlesticks have very small wicks, which can indicate that high and low prices for the time period did not move very much from the opening and closing price.

Hammers and Inverted Hammers

The next thing to learn about candlesticks is special types and patterns. Below, we see a hammer and an inverted hammer.

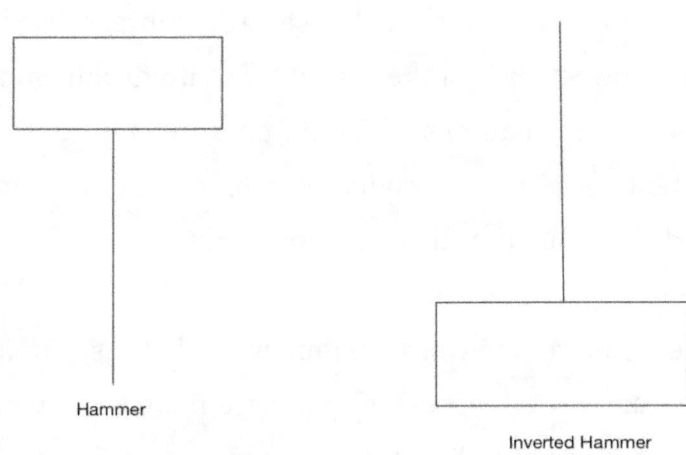

Hammer

Inverted Hammer

Picture 6

When an inverted hammer appears at the top of an upward trend, it can be called a shooting star. Looking at the hammer first, for the case of an increasing price, the opening and closing prices were pretty close in value. However, during the trading period, the price went to a level that was a bit lower. Then, there was a rebound to end up at higher prices by closing. This is an indication that while the bears (people pushing for low prices – in the case of Forex betting against the base currency) pushed prices down, by the end of the trading period the price was pushed back higher by the bulls (which in the case of Forex would be those hoping for the base currency to rise in price).

If the candlestick is a decreasing price candlestick, the meaning of a hammer is different. In that case, the price was pushed relatively low and it went back up for the trading period – higher than the lowest price of the period – but it failed to go above the opening price. A hammer of this nature could represent changing sentiment as the bulls could be gaining momentum, having pushed prices up after they hit a low point.

Now let's look at an inverted hammer. In that case, for a green or hollow candlestick representing a price increase, the price went up very high during the time period but was pushed back down by closing. That means during the time period the bulls were predominant, but by closing the bears had pushed prices down from the high that had been reached earlier.

For a price decrease, an inverted hammer or shooting star means that, although prices were pushed up high, the bears won out by the end of the time period and we ended up with a lower closing price. At the top of an uptrend, this is called a shooting star. A shooting star is an important signal to look for in your charts, as it may indicate a coming declining trend in price.

Aside: Understanding charts

Let's make sure that we understand charts and their meaning. First, you need to know the currency pair and which currency is the base currency and which currency is the secondary. If the trend in the chart is up, that means the base currency is favored. The price of the currency pair is increasing. If there is a downward trend in the chart, this means that the secondary currency is favored. That means the price of the currency pair is decreasing. Which situation is favorable depends on your position? If you bought a currency pair, this means you expected the price to move in favor of the base currency., for EUR/USD, if you bought the pair and the price is moving up on the chart, you are making money. If the price is moving down on the chart, you're losing money.

Now suppose that you sold the EUR/USD pair instead. If the price is dropping, you will buy the pair back to exit your position. That means you made a profit since you had sold it at a higher price. A decrease in the chart means the USD is gaining with respect to the Euro. On the other hand, a rising price means that if you have to exit your position, you're in for a loss, since you'd have to buy it back at a higher price.

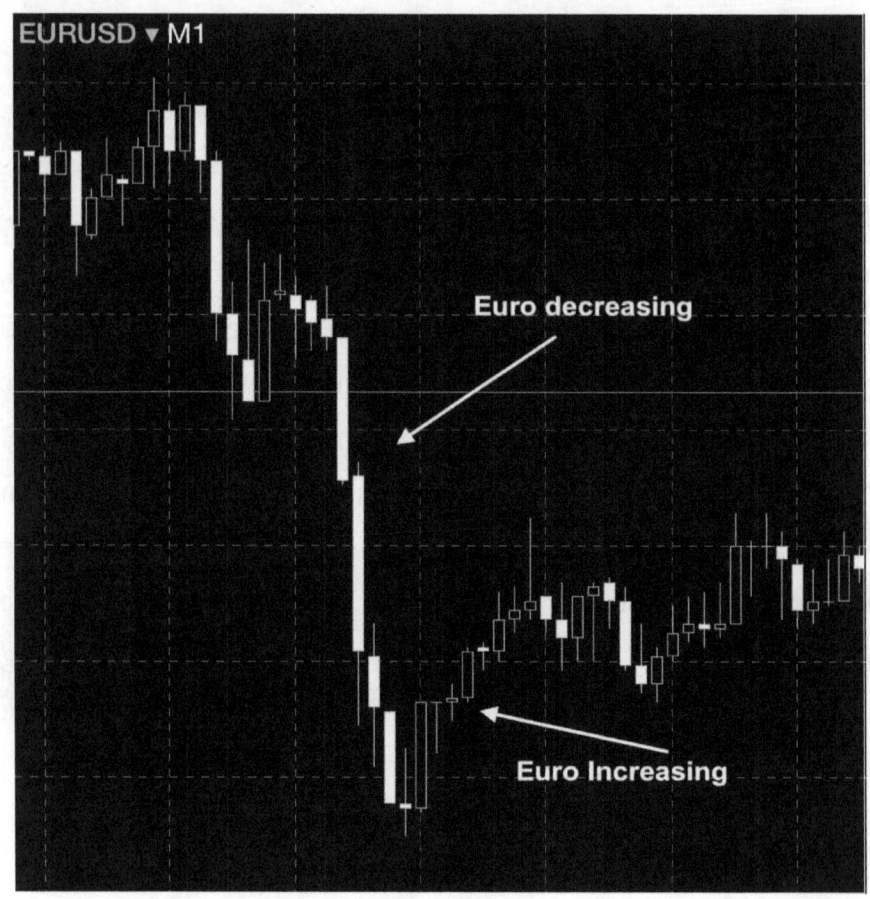

Picture 7

Charting Time Frames

When you do Forex charting, you'll see mysterious codes associated with the chart. These include M1, M5, M15, M30, H1, H4, D1, W1 and MN. This is simply the time frame displayed on the chart. Here M means "minute", H means "hour", D means "day", W means "week" and MN means "one month." The time frame of interest will depend on your trading style and strategies.

84

If you are scalping, then you're going to want a short time period, like M1. A swing trader will probably want W1 or even MN.

- M1: One Minute
- M5: Five Minutes
- M15: Fifteen Minutes
- M30: Thirty Minutes
- H1: One Hour
- H4: Four Hour
- D1: One Day
- W1: One Week
- MN: One Month

You can think of charting as zooming in or out with a microscope. The level of detail that you want to look at depends on your needs. If you are a swing or position trader, the information you get from zooming in isn't going to be all that helpful. If you're holding your trade for a week to a month, or over several months in the case of a position trader, then you're not really interested in the fluctuations in price that are happening over the course of 5 or 15 minutes of time.

It's important to be clear about the time frame that you are looking at and what an increasing or decreasing candle represents depending on the position that you hold on the currency pair.

Now, we are going to have a look at some important candle patterns that can indicate changing trends.

Engulfing Pattern

One of the most significant patterns you can see is called engulfing. This happens when a candlestick of a specific type is much larger than a candlestick of the opposite type that directly preceded it. This can indicate a significantly changing sentiment. If the engulfing candle is a price decrease or bearish candle, that indicates the sellers have overwhelmed the buyers and it signals a coming downtrend. If the engulfing candle is a price increase or bullish candle, that tells us that the buyers have overwhelmed the sellers and an uptrend is likely.

In the chart snapshot below, we see an engulfing pattern at the end of a downturn. A bearish or price decreasing candlestick is followed by a larger green or price increasing candlestick. We have pointed this out with the arrow. That means that traders are starting to buy the currency pair. In this case, after a lot of selling of the currency pair, favoring the USD since this is the EUR/USD pair, there was a strong change in the opposite direction where the price was pushed up higher. That means that there were a lot more buyers entering the market rather than sellers over the subsequent time period. You can see from the chart that this was followed by an increase in price.

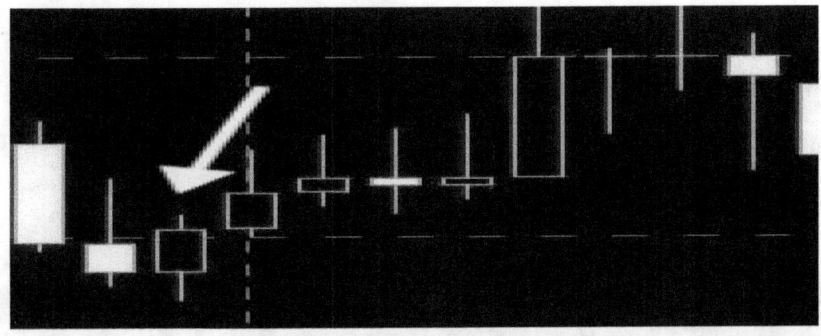

Picture 8

Tweezer Patterns

Tweezer patterns are important for traders that use scalping as their main strategy. If you are at the top of an uptrend, you are looking for two candles next to each other with long upper wicks that are about the same height. This indicates that in two time periods in a row, the price reached the same high, but there was a pullback from the high price. Tweezers are mostly interesting for short time frames, in particular, the M1/M5 or one- and five-minute-time frames. That is why they are mostly of interest for scalping traders who are interested in making profits off small moves over short time periods. A tweezer at the top of an uptrend represents a failure of the price to break resistance. You will want to see a green or bullish candle followed by a bearish candle to be sure it's a signal. The bearish candle indicates that the price was

87

pushed up to the same level the second time, but then it closed lower, indicating a coming downtrend.

If the tweezer pattern happens at the top of an uptrend, this is a signal that the price can't be pushed any higher. When prices can't be pushed any higher, this usually means that they are heading into a downward trend.

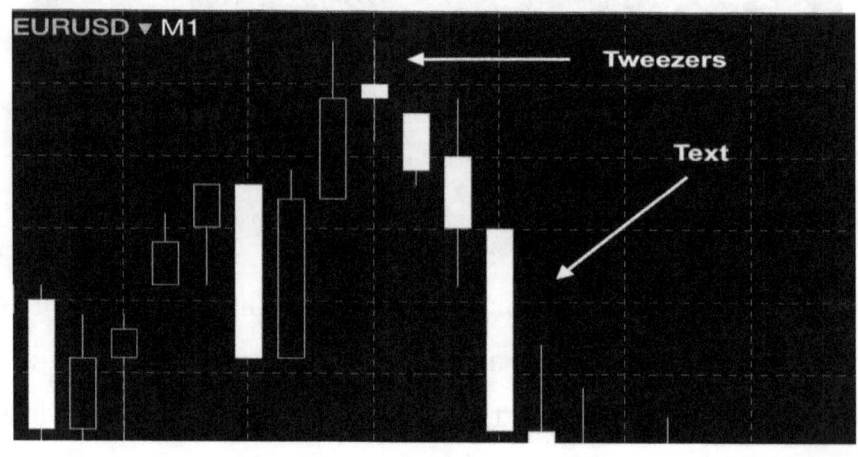

Picture 9

This can happen at the bottom of a trend as well, as we see in the chart below. When this happens at the bottom of a trend, the low price dropped to a specific low two time periods in a row and couldn't be pushed down any further. That indicates a coming uptrend and you can see in the chart this is what happened.

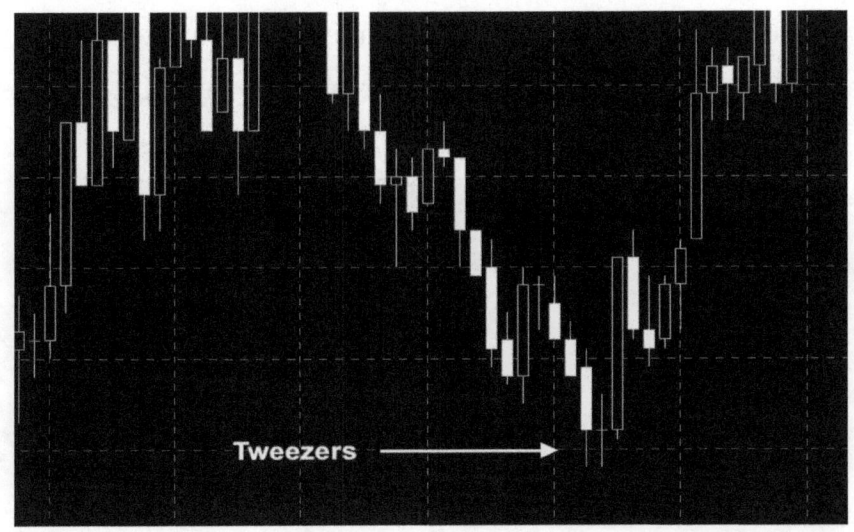

Picture 10

Doji Indecision Candles

Indecision candles are those that have narrow bodies and long wicks that are about the same length on both sides. What this means is that the price was pushed equally high and equally low during the time period, but the closing price ended up about where the opening price was. There was a lot of price action over the time period of interest, with prices being pushed way up high, then way down low by the same amount, but in the end, the price settled about where it had begun. There wasn't a clear victory for buyers or sellers during the time frame. At least for that moment, the market is not pushing one way or the other. In the image below, we show the ultimate indecision candle. Note the very long wicks and the extremely narrow candle body. That tells us that the opening and closing prices almost ended up exactly the same.

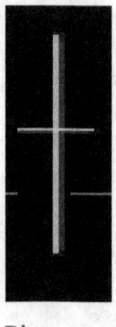

Picture 11

Three Inside Up or Three Inside Down

A three inside up pattern is formed by three candlesticks. The first candlestick will be a bearish candlestick at the bottom of a downtrend. This will be followed by a bullish candlestick. It does not need to be engulfing. However, it will be followed by a second bullish candlestick with a higher closing price. This indicates changing sentiment in the market and now buyers have overwhelmed sellers.

Although this can be a strong signal, keep in mind that it's suggesting and not proof of a coming uptrend.

Three inside down is the reverse that occurs at the top of an uptrend. In this case, you have a bullish candle. Then it's followed by a bearish candle and then a second bearish candle. In this case, the market sentiment is becoming negative (for the base currency) and a sell-off is about to begin. Usually, but not always, a downtrend will follow. In the example below, we see that there are two bearish candles in a row after the peak. That is followed by the downtrend. If you are looking to sell the currency pair, this would be a good time to do so.

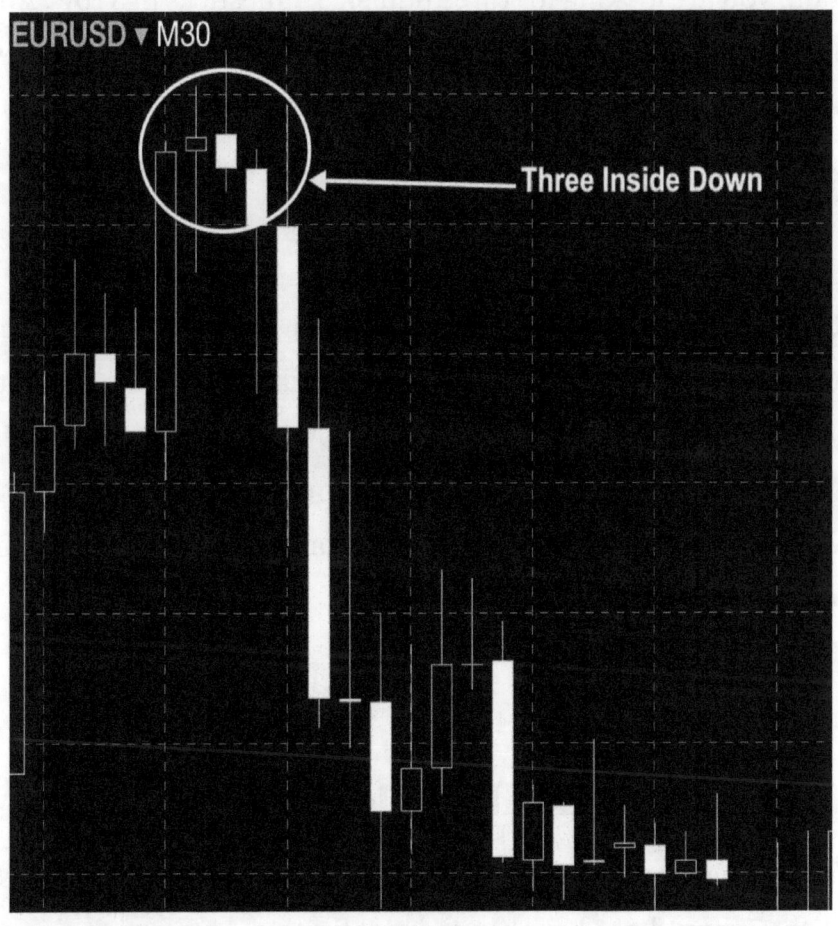

Picture 12

Three White Soldiers

This pattern refers to three bullish candlesticks in a row after a downtrend. The "white" color comes from the candlestick notation of the early days when bullish candlesticks were displayed on black and white charts with a hollow body. Today they should probably be called three green soldiers.

Again, you are looking for three bullish candlesticks in a row. And you're looking for them to occur during a downward trend. When you see three times in a row where the trading session ended with increasing prices at closing, this means that a coming uptrend is likely.

Of course, the converse can always happen. That is, you can be in an uptrend and then see three bearish candlesticks in a row. More than likely, that indicates a coming downward trend in prices, since we've seen three lower closing prices over three trading sessions in a row. Market sentiment has turned in favor of the secondary currency.

How to Use Candlestick Patterns

It's important to realize that candlestick patterns are suggestive, but they should not be taken to be definitive. In practice, a good trader is going to use candlestick patterns in conjunction with other tools. Normally what you want to do is look for signals of a coming change in trend and then confirm with other signals from different methods. In the next chapter, we are going to talk about the tools of technical analysis in more detail, which will include using moving averages in order to estimate coming changes in trends. A good trader, in this case, would be studying the candlesticks and note a signal, but that would also have moving averages on their charts and look for signals that confirm the information they see in the candlestick.

With that in mind, here are some suggestions of how candlestick patterns would be used. The first thing is you want to do is to catch a change in trend early. That means being on top of your candlestick charts. Second, you should be looking at relevant time frames. If you're looking to make a swing trade that will last several days, you are going to be looking at five minutes time intervals. And of course, the contrary also holds true. If scalping is your strategy, you wouldn't be looking at a one-day chart.

Let's look at the perspective of a buyer of a currency pair. If you're the buyer, obviously you were looking for price increases in order to profit. That means that people are buying up the primary currency of the pair., to enter your trades, you would actually be looking for downward trends. This can be a bit tricky. What you want to do is let a downward trend go down as much as possible.

As it's going down, you will be looking for any signals of a coming uptrend. Then once you spot a signal of an upcoming uptrend and you're able to confirm it using another method, you buy the currency pair. Then you're going to want to ride the wave upward as far as possible. When you start seeing signals of a coming down trend, it's time to sell your currency pair.

Smart and disciplined traders also use predetermined levels of profit and loss. We've mentioned this before, but you definitely want to stop loss in case your bet is wrong. This will help minimize potential losses that could happen with the trade. On most trading platforms, you will also see a take profit order that can be included when you make your trade. A take profit order is an automatic order that we'll execute when a certain level of profit is reached.

For those who are patient and not anxious to get out of the trade as quickly as possible, you can simply let your trade ride between your stop loss and your taking profit levels. To understand how this will work, we can take a look at the stock market.

If you're going to buy a stock and you simply place a buy order for a certain number of shares, you're doing what's called a market order. That means you'll buy the shares immediately at the market price, but it's possible to buy and sell shares using what's called a limit order. With a limit order, you specify that the trade is only executed if the market price matches the price you specify on the limit order. In the case of the stop-loss order, you set a low price that is acceptable to you for your level of loss. In the case of stocks maybe be $.50 a share, or a dollar per share. If the price drops level specified in the stop-loss order, the trade is automatically executed by the system.

You can also place automatic sell orders that occur at a higher pricing point. They work the same way, but in this case, you would set a higher price than what you paid for the stock. As an example, let's pretend that we purchase shares of stock for $50. We can place a limit order to sell the shares if the price reaches $60 a share.

So, if the price rises to $60 a share, the trade will be executed automatically, and we will get our $10 per share profit. Setting boundaries like this to exit the trades helps take emotion out of the equation. When big money is on the line, taking emotion out of the equation is an important factor in becoming a successful trader. You can be sure that more often than not-new traders and even experienced ones, are going to make serious mistakes when they start getting emotional about the trades. As we've said earlier, getting emotional can work both ways.

We want to approach our Forex trading in the same manner. Now, let's look at the case of someone betting against the currency pair. How are they going to use candlesticks? Someone who is selling a currency pair and so who is really hoping that the secondary currency is going to rise with respect to the primary, is analogous to someone shorting a stock. What that means, in practice, is that if you are betting that the secondary currency is going to rise in value, to look for a point to sell, you seek out peaks in price. Of course, it's easy to pick up the peaks after-the-fact. Doing so beforehand is a little bit more difficult, so we have to estimate when a trend is changing. That means for a small bit of time, you have to let the trends start to play out. Then, after a rise in prices of the currency pair, you look for signals of the coming downtrend. What you're going for, in this case, is to sell high and buy low., when you see signals on a becoming downtrend, you sell the currency pair. Then, you wait for the downtrend to play out and this can mean looking for definitive signals that the downtrend is about to reverse and becoming uptrend again, after that you buy the currency pair back. Of course, in this case, the traders are also going to use confirming signals from other indicators.

If you're selling currency pairs, it's also important to use the same practice for safety described above. That, of course, means that you're going to use a stop-loss order in conjunction with the take profit order.

You might notice that if you are using stop loss and take profit orders, this simplifies the use of candlestick charts. That's because we are only using the candlestick chart to find a good entry point for the trade. Once we've entered the trade, we let fate takes its course. We set our boundaries for the trade and accept the results no matter what they are. Sometimes you're going to miss those gems when the train keeps rising, but that's okay; the goal is to get sustainable profits. Sustainable profits can be multiplied by repeating the process over and over as the year goes on. Sometimes your guesses are going to be incorrect and you're going to lose a trade. Be ready for that possibility.

As useful as candlesticks are, putting some automatic trades in that, helps our odds significantly. That's because while candlesticks are good indicators, they don't always work out. If you aren't using the automatic buy and sell orders to exit the trade, that means you're going to be under pressure trying to decide the right time to exit the trade. You are going to be sitting there studying the candlesticks hoping to make the right exit. For some people, that kind of active analysis is really appealing. If that's you, you are certainly free to take your chances and do the analysis. But for most people, especially beginners, it's probably better to set up the automatic exit points.

Where to Set Take Profit and Stop-Loss Orders

If you remember earlier in the book, we discussed support and resistance. Support and resistance on the charts are where you're going to set your take profit and stop-loss orders. This is not going to be a perfect procedure because sometimes there is going to be a breakout. The breakout and going either direction, either favoring the primary or base currency or favoring the secondary currency. A breakout favoring the base currency will be a price increase. A breakout facing the secondary is going to be a price decrease for the pair.

So when you're making your trade and presumably beforehand actually, you have studied recent price trends for the currency pair. From that, you will have noticed the zone of resistance or the highest price that the currency pair has lately been able to reach. You should set your take profit level or price slightly below the resistance price. Chart patterns are actually chaotic in practice, therefore imagining that there is an ideal resistance price with a straight line is probably not going to happen. In the next chapter, we will talk about Bollinger bands, a tool that can be helpful in having the computer figure out support and resistance for you. But if you don't use Bollinger bands, then you have to estimate it manually. That will be imprecise of course, but it will set a pricing level so that you only sell when you make the amount of profit that you're looking for.

Similarly, the level of support would represent the price level to sell the currency pair. This will be done by setting a stop-loss order. This time you're going to set your stop loss price, slightly below the support level. How far below is going to be a personal decision and it's going to depend on how many lots and so forth that you have purchased.

Now, if you are selling the currency pair, you do the reverse: your resistance level is going to represent the price where you should buy the currency pair to exit the trade and minimize your losses. The support level will be the point at which you would buy the currency pair back in order to take profits. Then, you are probably going to set your take profit price level slightly above the support level and your stop loss price level slightly above the resistance price.

Chapter 9: Trading Indicators

The primary tools of technical analysis are the candlestick charts and indicators. Being a successful trader is, to a certain extent, about odds. It's impossible for anyone to know the future. In addition, there can be unexpected events like a sudden news release. If that happens, you can ruin your trade in the blink of an eye.

So, while we can't predict the future with absolute certainty, what we can do is increase the probability of success. The main way to do that is to incorporate multiple indicators together with your candlestick analysis. And then you want to use your take profit and stop-loss orders in order to ensure that your trade isn't destroyed by some unexpected move, no matter the source.

Now it's important to realize that despite the large array of available tools, you don't necessarily improve your position by using a huge number of them simultaneously. In other words, the more tools that you're using, the less attention you are going to be paying to the signals each tool is giving you. It's better to master a small number of tools and indicators to become a better trader. If I were a new trader, I would much rather be an expert at candlesticks, which means understanding all the possible patterns inside and out, than I would want to be in a situation where my understanding of candlesticks is shallow and I'm throwing a whole bunch of indicators on my charts. In the same way, it's important to know that while there are several indicators available, they are usually giving you the same information. It's better to take two or three indicators and use them with the candlestick charts for your technical analysis.

Moving Averages

The first indicator that we are going to look at is called a moving average. To calculate a moving average, the system looks at a past number of prices called periods. Depending on your timeframe, that is what the period is going to be., if you're looking at five-minute intervals (i.e., five-minute trading sessions), one period is going to be a five-minute interval. Therefore, if you take at nine-period moving average, it will take the prices for the past nine five-minute intervals and then calculate the average. The default on most charting Applications is to use closing price for each trading session in order to calculate the averages.

There are several different moving averages available. Some are more accurate than others and different traders have their own preferences. But let's look at the first case, which is called a simple moving average. What this does is to calculate a mean price for each point, along with the chart., at a given trading session if you have a nine-period simple moving average, it will start at the current trading session and add the closing price up with the closing prices of the eight previous training sessions. Then, it will divide the results by nine to give the average.

Okay, that is simple enough. Everyone understands that and you're probably wondering why I am going through the trouble of explaining it to that level of detail. The reason is you should observe what this kind of average does. The important thing to note is that a simple moving average is treating all prices equally. Let me ask you a question. Do you think that the price, nine training sessions ago, is as important as the price of the last trading session when trying to determine a trend? Obviously, the answer is no. Prices from long ago in training sessions have less relevance.

For this reason, people with mathematical minds have developed many different moving averages. The goal of developing more moving averages is to create moving averages that are more accurate. The most commonly used moving average that is more advanced is called an exponential moving average. We won't bother to get into the mathematical details of this; you can look it up online if it's interesting to you. But there is one key point that we need to know about the exponential moving average and what really makes it different from the simple moving average. The key to the difference is that the exponential moving averages weight prices. What happens is closing prices from more recent trading sessions have more weight, as compared to closing prices from trading sessions that ended further away in the past. This will help you get a more accurate picture because it's averaging the most recent closing prices more than using prices from 10, 20, or 200 trading sessions past.

There are even more complicated and to a certain degree, more accurate moving averages that have tried to expand on this kind of improvement. One of the most frequently used moving averages is called the Hull moving average. This moving average is named after its developer. Its details aren't really that important for most traders. What will be important is how moving averages are used in practice.

To find out which moving average you prefer to use, you should run some charts and then put the different moving averages on the chart. Then, just simply see which ones seem to suit your purposes. One thing that can be said, is that the more frequently you trade, or putting things another way, the shorter your time frame for exiting the trade, the more accurate you're moving averages should be. My personal opinion is that if you are scalping or day trading, a Hull or exponential moving average is far preferable to a simple moving average.

If you are swing trading, instead, or even position trading, a simple moving average might be sufficient. But even in the case of these longer time frames for making your trades, you are probably better off using at least exponential moving averages. It may be true and it probably is that if you survey 100 traders, you are going to find that every possible type of moving average is being used by someone. You might also find that there is a slight preference for one or the other. What these kinds of results would tell you is not really much. The main point when it comes to moving averages is that you should use some type of moving average indicator as part of your analysis. For the record, most Forex traders seem to prefer using exponential moving averages.

How to Use Moving Averages

The reason that we use moving averages is so that we can spot trend reversals. You will be using moving averages in conjunction with your candlestick analysis. A typical approach is to take a look at your candlestick charts and look for signs of a trend reversal, then you can check your moving averages and see if they confirm what the candlestick chart is telling you. However, trading platforms allow you to overlay moving averages on top of your charts. Hence, we can always have our moving averages on the chart so that we can look for the signals we seek in the candlesticks and the moving averages simultaneously. The more of a short-term trader that you are, the more important it is to be on top of the information. You need to move fast if you're a scalper or a day trader.

The way that moving averages are used is to compare or utilize two moving averages with different periods on the same chart. One moving average will be a short period moving average. Typically, a nine-period moving average is used for the short period option. For a long period, you can use different values, such as a 20-period moving average. There may be reasons to use different time frames, we could use a 20-period moving average, together with a 50-period average. Some traders will even use 200-period moving averages in their analysis.

What are we looking for was moving averages?

The key pattern that we seek when we must move averages on the chart is for the short-term moving average to cross the long-term moving average. This is the signal that there is a coming trend reversal. There are only two things that you need to look for; The first is called a golden cross. The jargon people use isn't really relevant, but there is a reason it's called golden. This is associated with a short period moving average crossing above a long period moving average. This is an indication that the trend in price is going to be increasing. That's why it's called golden, but that name probably comes from applications of moving averages on the stock market. Remember, on Forex you may be hoping for a decrease in price since you are looking at pairs rather than individual securities.

Let's take the perspective of being a buyer of a currency pair. That means we want the primary or base currency to increase in value concerning the secondary currency. Therefore, we are looking for price increases for the currency pair. I just want to review that information to make sure everyone has that straight in their mind. When you are brand-new to Forex, the distinctions can be a little bit confusing so please, bear with me if you're one of the lucky people that completely understand how things are working.

in case you are a buyer of a currency pair, you're going to use a short period moving average crossing over a long period moving average as a buying signal. But like candlesticks, you shouldn't use any indicator in isolation. You will want to confirm the signal elsewhere. One way to do this is to simply match it up with what the candlesticks are telling you. Alternatively, there are other indicators you can use to confirm the signal.

Now let's take the contrary position such that you are selling the currency pair, in the hopes that the secondary currency is going to be the one that is increasing in value. That means for the currency pair as a whole; you are hoping the price is going to decrease so that you can buy the currency pair back and make a profit. When you see the short period moving average crossing over a long period moving average, it's actually a sell signal.

However, the astute observer will note that in both cases a short period moving average crossing above a long period moving average, is a signal to answer your position.

Now let's consider the opposite situation. That is, in this case, we have a short period moving average, which is crossing below the long period moving average. On the stock market, they call this the death cross. It's a strong indicator that a calming downturn in prices has been reached. Once again if you see this type of crossing pattern, you don't want to get too anxious. What you want to do is confirm the signal based on what the other indicators and candlesticks may be telling you.

With that in mind, let's look at how you would proceed based on the signal. As usual in the first case, we will take the position of the buyer of a currency pair. In this case, if you have not gotten into a position, you're going to take the signal as an indicator that you should be paying attention for signals that suggest a good time to enter a new position.

If you have already bought the currency pair, this is a signal that it's time to exit your position. You should immediately sell your currency pair in order to take your profits.

Now, we'll take the position of being a seller of a currency pair. Our bet is, once again, on the secondary currency. If you see the short period moving average crossing below the long period moving average, that's a signal to answer your position by selling the currency pair. The hope here is that you are going to be selling the currency pair when the price is high. Then, you're going to watch the trend, looking for the converse situation to occur, which is another uptrend signal. In that case, you would buy back the currency pair and take your profits since you purchased it back at a lower price.

In the chart below, we see two moving averages in the bottom graph. The green moving average is a 10-period exponential moving average and the red line is a 20-period exponential moving average. The actual pricing chart is shown at the top of the chart. Notice that when the green line crosses above the red line, there is an increase in prices. This is for the EUR/USD currency pair, so that would indicate that the Euro is strengthening relative to the dollar. You will also notice that when the green line crosses below, that is the short period moving average crosses below the long period moving average, the price declines.

Of course, you could look at this situation from the other perspective. That is any time that you see the longer period moving average crossing above the short period moving average; this indicates a coming drop for decreasing trend in price.

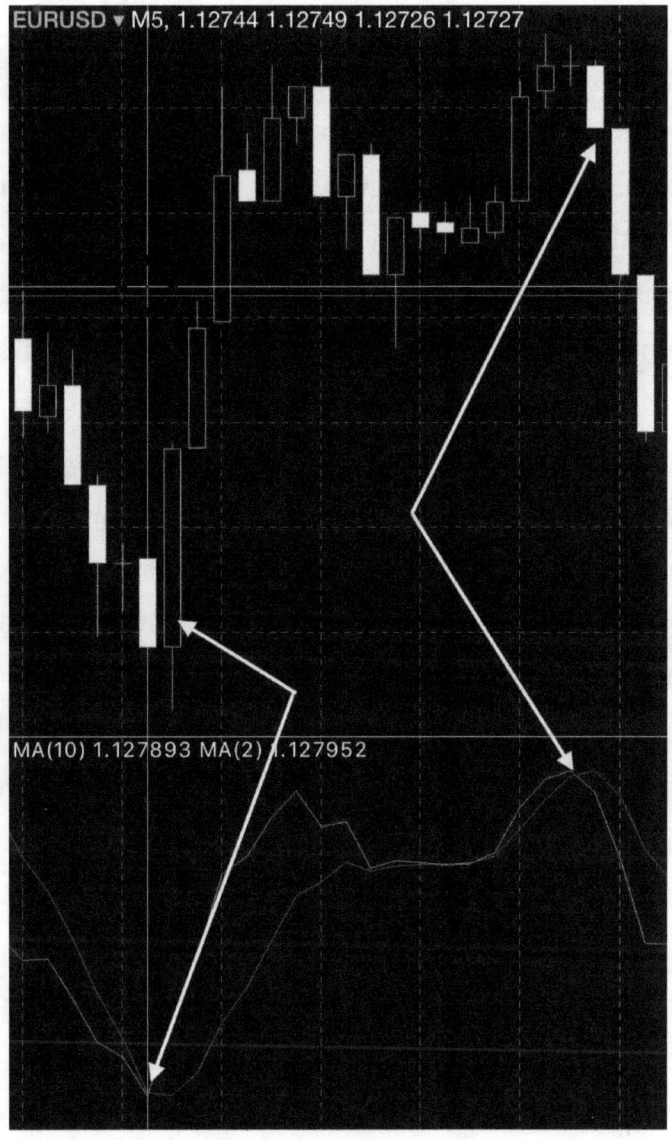

Picture 13

This example is a good one to look at because we can zoom in and check the candlesticks. Draw your attention to the first crossing where the green line goes above the red line, that is the short period moving average is crossing over the long period moving average. To review that should be an indicator that the pricing trend is going to increase. Of course, we see that's what happened in the chart. But what we want to do is zoom in here and look at the candlesticks. And indeed, you can see at the exact point where are the moving averages cross; there is a very large engulfing green or bullish candle that follows the bearish or white candle that appeared at the bottom of the downtrend.

This example is a perfect one to illustrate how you would use this type of information. Notice that the indicator from the moving averages happens a little bit before the change in the candlesticks. However, the candlesticks confirm the signal. Having that matchup is a strong situation that you would be making the right trade if you use those signals to enter or exit your positions as appropriate.

We also see the same confirmation on the right side of the chart. Notice that in the bottom chart for the graph, the red line crosses over the green line. In other words, the short period moving average dips below the long period moving average at that point. This, of course, would be a signal of the downtrend. Now turn your attention to the candles at the top of the chart. This one sticks out like a sore thumb; you notice there are three white or bearish candlesticks in a row, each with declining closing prices. Once again we have a good example of confirmation using the moving averages and the candlesticks.

RSI

The next indicator we are going to look at is called the Relative Strength Index, or RSI. Many trading platforms have this on their charts by default. You use the Relative Strength indicator to determine whether a market is overbought or oversold. Let's explore what those terms mean.

If a market is oversold, that means too many people have sold their positions. In the case of a currency pair on Forex, this would mean that the secondary currency has actually gotten too to the primary currency. But you can still say it's an oversold signal because people are selling the currency pair to favor the secondary currency. The Relative Strength Index ranges between zero and 100. Be cut off, is usually used in order to indicate oversold conditions, is when the Relative Strength Index drops below 30. If this happens and the market is oversold, it should indicate a coming trend reversal. At the very least, it would indicate that the prices are not going to continue dropping.

Therefore, if you had sold the currency pair because you thought the secondary would increase in proportion or against the primary, this would be a strong signal that you should buy back your position.

On the other hand, if you are interested in betting on the primary currency, oversold conditions could be a good signal to buy the currency pair. This would be done under the assumption that the overall trend would reverse and we would be soon witnessing an increase in prices.

The relative strength indicator is also used to look for overbought conditions. When financial security is overbought, this means we are expecting it has risen as far as it's going to go in price. Therefore, overbought conditions indicate that the price is going to start dropping in the near future.

For the relative strength indicator, if the value goes above 70, this is taken as a signal of overbought conditions. Let's look at how we would handle it.

First, let's consider the bullish investor. That is the trader has purchased the currency pair in anticipation that the base currency is going to rise in price. In this situation, if you see an RSI above

70, this could be an indicator that you should exit your position by selling the currency pair.

If you hadn't taken a position at all, you still would pay attention even if you were looking to bet on the base currency. Although it would be a little bit far off, this would draw your attention the fact that prices are going to drop and so an opportunity to enter a position at a low price might be presenting itself in the near future.

Now we consider it is the opposite situation. This time you are betting on the secondary currency. In that case, an overbought situation is an opportunity to sell the currency pair. When a currency pair is overbought if you are looking for gains in the secondary currency, that is an opportunity to enter your position. People can get seduced by the RSI. They can also get seduced by the many other indicators that you can add to your charts. But it's important to take them all with a grain of salt. I hate to be repetitive, but this is very important. What this means is what we want to do is utilize the tools that are available to the fullest extent possible. But in every case, you want to confirm what the indicator is telling you before you act. As we saw in the last section, using candlestick charts to confirm is an excellent way to proceed.

Bollinger Bands

The last major indicator that we are going to consider is called *Bollinger bands*. This is a very powerful indicator, especially when prices are bouncing around in between a limited range. Bollinger bands give you three pieces of information. The first is a 20-period moving average. This is going to form a central line within the bands. The bottom band is going to be defined by a low-price level which is calculated to be two standard deviations below the mean. You can think of the bottom band as defining the level of price supports at any given time. When you're going to use price supports as a factor in deciding when to trade, where to put your stop-loss, or where to take profits, this is a good way to do it without relying on your own analysis of the charts.

The second band is found above the moving average. This is also calculated to be two standard deviations above the mean. Therefore, you can take this to be resistance. Then, this would be the upper pricing level that you would expect shortly. Again, it can be used in the way you would use resistance. Therefore, it can be used in order to defined points to enter or exit trades. It would be also used for a take profit pricing level if you are buying a currency pair, or setting a stop loss for those that are selling the currency pair.

People also use the relative positions of the candlesticks with respect to the Bollinger bands to determine price reversals. You will look for candlesticks touching levels of support and resistance, that is looking for the candlesticks to touch outside Bullinger bands., if you see the candlesticks touching the upper Bullinger band and sometimes they will even go outside of it, that could be a signal of a coming price reversal heading downwards.

Conversely, if you see the candlesticks touching the lower Bollinger band curve, or going below it, that can also be a signal of importance. In this case, it would indicate a coming rise in prices.

Bollinger bands are one of the more advanced indicators available. As you can see, it's providing you three things in one. As such, the information that I've just given you tends to be fairly accurate. You should also note that Bollinger bands can also be set up using different metrics. When you add a Bollinger band to your charts, you have choices about which moving average to use. You can also determine how many standard deviations to use for the upper and lower curves. The default is to use a 20-period moving average in most cases, together with two standard deviations. There are good reasons to use this approach. Over short time periods, although there can certainly be a big price moves, it's relatively unlikely that prices are going to be following outside of the two standard deviation range. Using three standard deviations would be far too lenient.

And conversely, using one standard deviation would be extremely conservative. Maybe if you were scalping, one standard deviation could be a consideration so that you could take profit on small price moves. At the same time, it might constrain you too much so that you are taking profit at levels that are too small to overcome the spread.

Summary

In this chapter, we have summarized some of the most important and widely used indicators in the Forex industry. It's important to note that there are many more indicators then we've described here. Unfortunately, there just isn't enough space to discuss them all. But to be completely honest, it's unclear that devoting attention to all the indicators that are out there is worthwhile. As we mentioned at the outset, it turns out that all the different indicators are often giving you the same information. The best advice for a beginning trader is to stick with the small number of indicators and don't worry about all the rest. As we said earlier, it's better to become thoroughly acquainted with two or three indicators, then it is to be using a half-dozen indicators and not really understand what you're doing. I even take that position when it comes to expert traders. You should keep things simple and focus on what the data is telling you.

If we had to give advice, here is what they would be: the first is that you should master candlestick charts. We have given you a general overview in this book and that's good enough information to get started. But if you want to be a successful trader, we highly recommend that you take some time to find more in-depth discussions focusing on candlestick charts alone. You should learn all the patterns that are known to occur, which indicate the coming trend reversals. You should study them thoroughly so that you recognize them on sight.

Second, you won't be surprised to learn that I am going to recommend using the indicators that we have discussed in this chapter. For moving averages, my preference is to use exponential moving averages. To determine the periods used, I suggest doing a little more independent research so that you can see the advantages and disadvantages of using different combinations. No matter what you choose, what's going to happen is you're going to combine a longer period and a short period moving average. I also like the Hull moving average as well, but stick to the exponential. No reason to confuse things. Again, I want to emphasize that the reason I personally make this choice is that I don't want a moving average that gives misleading information by giving equal weight to priced closings from trading sessions that happened a long time ago.

The second tool that you can incorporate is RSI. I simply check its value periodically whenever I'm looking for a trend change. But I don't focus on it too heavily.

Finally, Bollinger bands are extremely useful. These can be used in a supportive role, in my opinion. The main reason that I use them is to identify the pricing levels that are two standard deviations out from the mean. Then these can be used to determine entry and exit points on trades, that is stop-loss order points and take profit pricing levels. But I don't focus on these bands all that much, to be honest. In practice, I mostly focus on simply using moving averages and crossings, along with the candlestick charts.

Chapter 10: Tips, Tricks and Errors to Avoid

Now we'll turn our attention to giving some tips, tricks and advice on errors to avoid in order to ensure as much as possible that you have a successful time trading.

Avoid the Get Rich Quick Mentality

Any time that people get involved with trading or investing, the hope is always there that there's a possibility of the big winning trade. It does happen now and then. But quite frankly, it's a rare event. In many occasions, even experienced traders are guessing wrong and taking losses. It's important to approach Forex for what it really is. It's a business. It is not a gambling casino even though a lot of people treated that way so you need to come to your Forex business—and it is a business no matter if you do it part-time, or quit your job and devote your entire life to it—with the utmost seriousness. You wouldn't open a restaurant and recklessly buy 1 thousand pounds of lobster without seeing if customers were coming first. So, why would you approach Forex as if you were playing slots at the casino? Take it seriously and act as if it's a business because it really is. Again, it doesn't matter if you officially create a corporation to do your trades or not, it's still a business no matter what. That means you should approach things with care and avoid the get rich quick mentality. The fact is the get rich quick mentality never works anywhere. Unfortunately, I guess I could say I've been too strong in my assertion. It does work on rare occasions. It works well enough that it keeps the myth alive. But if we took 100 Forex traders who have to get rich quick mentality, my bet is within 90 days, 95% of them would be completely broke.

Trade Small

Our second tip has been placed right below the previous section because this tip is the antidote to falling prey to the get rich quick mentality. You should always trade small and set small achievable goals for your trading. The first benefit to trading small is that this approach will help you avoid a margin call. Second, it will also help you set profit goals that are small and achievable. That will help you stay in business longer.

Simply put, you will start gaining confidence and learning how to trade effectively if you get some trades that make $50 profits, rather than shooting for a couple of trades that would make thousands of dollars in one shot, but and up making you completely broke. Again, treat your trading like a real business. If you were opening a business, chances are you would start looking for slow and steady improvements and you certainly would not hope to get rich quick.

Let's get specific. Trading small means never trading standard lots. Even if you have enough cash to open an account such that you could trade standard lots, I highly recommend that you stay away from them. The large amount of capital involved and margin that would be used could just get you into a lot of financial trouble. For beginners, no matter how much money you are able to devote to your trading, I recommend that you start with micro lots. Take some time and learn how to trade with the small lots and start building your business earnings small profits at a time. Trading only with micro lots will help in force discipline and help you avoid getting into trouble. Make a commitment only to use micros for the first 60 days. After that, if you have been having decent success, consider trading a mini lot. You should be extremely cautious for the first 90 days in general.

Be careful with leverage

As we said earlier, the large leverage that you can get while Forex trading is a double-edged sword. Obviously, it's extremely beneficial. It allows you to enter and trades that would otherwise not be possible. On the other hand, the temptation is there to use all your leverage in the hopes of making it big on one or two trades. You need to avoid using up all your leverage. Remember that you can have a margin call and get yourself into big trouble if your trades go bad. And it's important to remember there's a high probability that some of your trades are going to go bad no matter how carefully you do all your analysis.

Not Using a Demo Account

A big mistake the beginners make, is jumping in too quickly. There is a reason that most broker-dealers provide demos or simulated accounts. If you don't have a clue what that reason is, let's go ahead and stated here. Brokers provide demo accounts because Forex is a high-risk trading activity. It can definitely be something that provides a lot of rewards and it does for large numbers of traders. But there is a substantial risk of losing your capital. Many beginners are impatient hoping to make money right away. That's certainly understandable, but you don't want to fall into that trap. Take 30 days to practice with a demo account. This will provide several advantages. Trading on Forex is different than trading on the stock market. Using the demo account, you can become familiar with all the nuances of Forex trading. This includes everything from studying the charts, to placing your orders and, most importantly, understanding both pips and margin. The fact that there is so much leverage available means you need to learn how to use it responsibly. You need to know how to experience going through the process and reading the available margin and so forth on your trading platform while you are actually trying to execute trades. A demo account let you do this without risking real capital. It is true that it's not a perfect simulation. The biggest argument against demo accounts is that they don't incorporate the emotion that comes with trading and real money. As we all know, it's those emotions, including panic, fear and greed, that lead to bad decisions. However, in my opinion, that is a weak argument against using demo accounts. The proper way to approach it is to use a demo account for 30 days and then spend 60 to 90 days doing nothing but trading micro lots. Don't worry, as your micro trading lots you can increase the number of your trades and earn profits. While I know you're anxious to get started, keeping yourself from losing all your money is a good reason to practice for 30 days before doing it for real.

Failing to Check Multiple Indicators

There is also a temptation to get into trades quickly just on a gut level hunch. You need to avoid this approach at all costs. Some beginners will start learning about candlesticks and then when they first start trading, they will recognize a pattern on a chart. Then in the midst of the excitement, they will enter a large trade based on what they saw. And then they will end up on the losing end of a trade. Some people are even worse and they don't even look at the candlesticks. Instead, they just look at the trend and think they better get in on it and they got all anxious about doing so. Then the trend suddenly reverses and they lose all their money so take seriously those two last chapters. That means first checking the candlesticks and then confirming at least with the moving average before entering or exiting a position. You should also have the RSI handy and you may or may not want to use Bollinger bands.

Use Stop Loss and Take Profit Orders

Well, I hate to repeat myself yet again, but this point is extremely important. I am emphasizing it over and over because it's one of the tools that you can use in order to protect yourself from heavy losses. One of the ways that you can get out of having to worry about margin calls and running out of money is to put stop-loss orders every time you trade. This will require studying the charts more carefully. You need to have a very clear idea where you want to get out of the trade, if it doesn't go in the direction you hoped. But if you have a stop-loss order in place, then you can avoid the problem of having your account just go down the toilet. Secondly, although the temptation is always there to look for as many profits as possible, in most cases, you should opt to set a take profit order when you make your trade. That way you set as we said, distinct boundaries which will ensure that you make some profit without taking too much risk. The problem with doing it manually is that excitement and greed will put you in a position where are you miss the boat entirely. What inevitably happens, is people get too excited hoping to earn more profits and they stay in the trade too long. The Forex market changes very fast and so what eventually happens is people that stay into long inevitably and up with a loss. Or at the very least they end up missing out on profits.

There is one exception to this point. There are some times when there is a distinct and relatively long-term upward trend. If you find yourself, by doing the analysis and determining that such an upward trend is here, that might be an exception to the rule. In that case, you want to try to ride the trend and maximize your profits.

Remember Price Changes Are in Pips

Beginners often make the mistake of forgetting about pips. If you have trouble with pips and converting them to actual money, go back and review the examples we provided. Remember that pips play a central role in price changes, you need to know your dollar value per pip in order to keep tabs on your profit and losses. This is also important for knowing the right stop loss and take profit orders to execute.

Don't Try Too Many Strategies or Trading Styles at Once

When you are a beginning Forex trader, it can be tempting to try everything under the sun. That can be too much for a lot of people. The most advisable thing to do is to stick with one strategy so don't try scalping and being a position trader at the same time. The shorter the time frame for your trades, the more time and energy, you have to put into each trade. Scalping and day trading are activities that would require full-time devotion. They are also high-pressure and that can help enhance emotions involved in the trades. For that reason, I don't really recommend those styles or strategies for beginners. In my opinion and to be honest it's mine alone, I think position trading is also too much for a beginner. It requires too much patience.

Perhaps the best strategy to use when you're beginning Forex trading is to become a swing trader. It's a nice middle ground, in between the most extremely active trading styles and something that is going to try people's patience such as position trading. When you do swing trading, you can do time periods longer than a day certainly, but as long or short as you need to meet your goals otherwise. Swing trading also takes off some of the pressure. And it gives you more time to think and react.

This does not mean that you can't become a scalper or day trader at some future date. What I am advising is that you gain some experience using more relaxed trading styles before taking that path. And believe me, swing trading is going to be challenging enough.

Don't Panic

One of the most natural results that happen in a trading environment is that when the inevitable thing happens—that is losing on a trade —panic sets in. Since you can end up losing a whole bunch of money and having your account closed and wiped out, it's reasonable to feel strong emotions when there are trades going bad. It's important to stay level-headed and know when to exit trades. But if you've read through all the advice that we've given, you shouldn't find yourself in a situation where you find yourself panicking in the first place. Ultimately this is going to be up to you. Are you disciplined enough to make sure that you have your stop-loss order in place? If you are going to take a cavalier attitude for thinking that you can't control the situation, history shows that, as a beginner, the odds are against you. That's why you should use the tools that the brokerage has provided not only to protect itself from the losses it would have to cover if your trades go wrong, but also to protect your own account and reputation. Panic puts you at risk for making the wrong decisions. Not only are we concerned about losing all our money and getting a margin call, my concern for you is also that you are going to exit a trade prematurely. Pricing charts are always chaotic. Sometimes they are going to dip in a little bit below where we would like, but then they are going to bounce up again. This is where panic actually takes most of its toll when people fear that they are going to lose everything and so they exit their position too early.

Conclusion

Thank you for taking the time to read this book and make it to the very end!

It is my sincere hope that you have found this book very informative. Forex trading is a very exciting path that can be used to build a fun and lucrative business. While it certainly carries risk, we have provided all the information that you need in order to trade as carefully as possible. If you learn from your mistakes and avoid taking reckless risks, forex trading could help you generate wealth over time and if you build slowly and carefully with an eye to the future, there is a real possibility that Forex trading can become a full-time business for you, allowing you to quit your so-called day job.

Thank you again for reading the book and I hope that you will visit our Amazon page and leave a constructive review. I always like to hear from my readers!

By the same Author:

HOW TO TRADE FOR A LIVING
7-DAY CRASH COURSE FOR BEGINNERS
SECRET STRATEGIES, TIPS AND TRICKS

OPTIONS TRADING

0.3045

MARK STOCK

HOW TO SWING TRADE FROM A-Z
7-DAY CRASH COURSE FOR BEGINNERS
PROVEN STRATEGIES, MONEY MANAGEMENT AND TRADING TOOLS

SWING
TRADING

MARK STOCK

A COMPREHENSIVE GUIDE FOR BEGINNERS
STRATEGIES TO MAXIMIZE SHORT-TERM TRADING AND MAKE BIG PROFITS

SWING TRADING
WITH OPTIONS

MARK STOCK

SWING TRADING
FOR BEGINNERS

A COMPREHENSIVE BEGINNER'S GUIDE
PROVEN STRATEGIES, MONEY MANAGEMENT
AND TRADING TOOLS

MARK STOCK

OPTIONS TRADING
FOR BEGINNERS

HOW TO TRADE FOR A LIVING
7 DAY CRASH COURSE:
SECRET STRATEGIES, TIPS AND TRICKS

MARK STOCK

www.ingramcontent.com/pod-product-compliance
Lightning Source LLC
Chambersburg PA
CBHW060904170526
45158CB00001B/485